Stock Price Predictions: A   Introduction to Probabilistic

Copyright

Copyright © 2023 by Azhar ul Haque Sario

Published by Azhar ul Haque Sario

azhar.sario@hotmail.co.uk

Table of Contents

Foreword

Welcome to "Stock Price Predictions: An Introduction to Probabilistic Models", an in-depth exploration of the complex world of stock market prediction models. This book serves as a comprehensive guide for both beginners and experienced investors, offering a detailed study of both traditional and modern methods used to forecast stock prices.

In the initial section, "Traditional Approaches", we explore common techniques for predicting share prices, including Fundamental Analysis, Technical Analysis, and Quantitative Analysis. We delve into more specialized methods like Sentiment Analysis, Time Series Analysis, and Machine Learning Algorithms, providing a thorough understanding of each process and their respective pros and cons.

In the second part, "Understanding the World of Probability-Based Models", we step into the intriguing world of probability models. This section introduces a broad spectrum of models like ARIMA, GARCH, VAR, MGARCH, Stochastic Volatility Models, and many more. Each model's functionality and application in estimating future share prices is explained thoroughly, creating an excellent resource for anyone looking to delve deeper into probability-based models for stock price predictions.

The final segment, "Instances of Successful Forecasts Using Probability-Based Models", illustrates successful real-world forecasts using these models. This includes well-recognized models like the Black-Scholes Model, Monte Carlo Simulations, Brownian Motion Model, ARIMA, and GARCH Model. The book wraps up with a look at the success of newer models like LSTM and Facebook's Prophet.

What sets "Stock Price Predictions: An Introduction to Probabilistic Models" apart from other books in this genre is its practical approach. In addition to explaining theories, it presents real-world examples of successful implementations. This book is an all-encompassing guide, providing the theoretical knowledge and practical skills required to navigate the intricacies of stock price predictions. Whether you're a novice investor or an experienced financial analyst, this book is an invaluable addition to your investment resources.

Factors Influencing Stock Prices

Share or equity prices, also known as stock prices, reflect the value of a company's shares traded in the stock market. The cost of a share is primarily dictated by the supply and demand dynamics in the stock market. If demand for a particular share rises, so does its price, and vice versa. The stock market functions like an auction, where buyers and sellers negotiate prices. Stocks are typically bought and sold in 100-share increments called "round lots", while any other quantity of shares is referred to as an "odd lot". The last traded price of a stock is usually the price reported on financial websites and news.

Various internal and external factors can influence stock prices. Internal factors include company financial performance, leadership shifts, product launches, and mergers and acquisitions. External factors can include economic changes, market sentiment, political developments, and global events.

A company's financial performance heavily impacts its stock price. A company with profits exceeding expectations will likely see its stock price increase, while disappointing profits could lead to a price drop. Financial metrics like earnings per share (EPS), price-to-earnings (P/E) ratio, and return on equity (ROE) are commonly used to assess a company's profitability.

Corporate developments and news can significantly sway a company's stock price. For example, the announcement of a merger or the launch of a new product can cause stock prices to fluctuate depending on investor reactions.

Market sentiment, or the overall investor attitude towards a specific security or financial market, significantly influences stock prices. Positive investor sentiment can drive up prices, while negative sentiment can cause prices to drop.

Economic indicators like GDP growth, inflation, unemployment rate, and interest rates can also impact stock prices. For example, rising interest rates can depress stock prices by making borrowing more expensive for companies, which may affect their profitability.

Political events and policies can also affect stock prices, as changes in tax laws, trade policies, or regulations can impact a company's profitability and consequently its stock price.

Global events like wars, pandemics, or natural disasters can create market uncertainty, leading to volatile stock prices. These events can also disrupt supply chains and negatively impact company operations and profitability.

Analysts and investors use methods like technical analysis and fundamental analysis to forecast future stock prices. Technical analysts use historical market data, primarily price and volume, to predict future price trends. Fundamental analysts, on the other hand, analyze a company's financial health, industry position, and market conditions to estimate its inherent value.

Dividends, earnings portions distributed to shareholders, can also influence stock prices. A high dividend payout can attract income-seeking investors, potentially driving up the stock price. Institutional investors like mutual funds and pension funds can also affect stock prices through their buying or selling of large quantities of shares. Finally, it's important to recognize that stock prices can sometimes fluctuate based on rumors, speculation, and market manipulation, which can lead to price bubbles and crashes, posing risks to individual investors.

Importance of Accurate Stock Predictions

Accurately forecasting stock prices is crucial in investment practices, not only for profit-making purposes but also for strategic planning, risk management, and overall financial stability. The importance of precise stock price prediction cannot be emphasized enough as it directly influences the investment choices of individuals, companies, and even governments. Having an accurate prediction of stock prices enables investors to make informed decisions about which stocks to buy, retain, or sell. It assists them in effectively planning their investment strategies and maximizing their returns. Incorrect predictions can result in significant losses, negatively impacting the investor's financial health.

Furthermore, the prediction of stock prices is essential in portfolio management, helping to create a balanced portfolio capable of enduring market volatility. An accurate forecast can guide investors in correctly distributing their funds among various assets, reducing the risk of overconcentration in a specific security or sector.

Accurate stock price prediction also encourages market efficiency. It ensures that stock prices accurately reflect their true intrinsic value, which aids in preventing speculative bubbles and market crashes, thereby contributing to the overall stability and integrity of the financial markets. For financial analysts and investment advisors, accurately predicting stock prices is vital. Their reputation, credibility, and client trust depend on it. Their forecasts are frequently used as a basis for investment decisions by individuals and institutional investors.

Precise stock price prediction also aids in better capital budgeting. Corporations depend on these predictions to make decisions about fundraising, capital expenditure, mergers and acquisitions, and other strategic initiatives. Incorrect predictions can lead to sub-optimal decisions, negatively affecting the company's financial position and growth prospects.

From a macroeconomic viewpoint, accurate stock price prediction is crucial for monetary policy decisions. Central banks track stock market trends to assess the economy's health and determine their policy actions. Misjudgments could lead to inappropriate policy decisions, potentially destabilizing the economy.

Moreover, predicting stock prices is critical for financial risk management. Banks, insurance companies, and other financial institutions use these predictions to assess their market risk and determine their risk mitigation strategies. Any inaccuracies could expose these institutions to higher risk levels, threatening their solvency and the stability of the financial system as a whole.

Accurate stock price prediction also contributes to financial research and education. Researchers use these predictions to test their theories and models, while educators use them to teach financial concepts and techniques. Misleading predictions could lead to flawed research findings and misconceptions among students.

In the age of algorithmic trading, the importance of accurate stock price prediction has increased significantly. These technologies heavily depend on these predictions to execute their trading strategies. Any inaccuracies could result in substantial trading losses, undermining the effectiveness and credibility of these technologies.

Lastly, accurate stock price prediction acts as a confidence-building measure for investors. It reassures them about the markets' fairness and transparency, encouraging them to invest more. This, in turn, promotes market liquidity and economic growth.

Probabilistic Models in Financial Analysis

Probabilistic models are key tools in the realm of finance and economics, providing mathematical predictions of outcomes by incorporating random variables. Fundamental to risk management, portfolio optimization, derivative pricing, and many other financial operations, these models account for the inherent uncertainty and randomness of financial markets. This uncertainty may arise from market volatility, economic shifts, or geopolitical events. Through these models, analysts can gauge the probability of different outcomes and make educated decisions. To create a probabilistic model, financial analysts first need to identify the random variables, which can range from stock prices and interest rates to inflation rates and currency exchange rates. The association between these variables is then mathematically defined, typically through statistical distributions. The assignment of probabilities to these variables is an essential phase in developing these models. These probabilities are determined based on historical data, expert opinion, or a blend of both, with the aim to accurately depict the real-world probability of each variable's potential outcomes. Once the variables and their probabilities are set, the model can simulate different scenarios, often via Monte Carlo methods. These methods involve repeated random sampling of the variables to generate a variety of outcomes. The outcomes produced by a probabilistic model offer valuable insights into potential risks and rewards. For instance, in portfolio management, these models can calculate the likelihood of achieving a specific return or the risk of a substantial loss, guiding investment decisions.

Probabilistic models are also crucial in derivative pricing, as options, futures, and other derivatives are all priced based on the probability of different market conditions. These models offer a systematic method to estimate these probabilities and therefore, the fair value of these financial instruments.

However, probabilistic models are not foolproof. They depend on the presumption that future probabilities will reflect past behavior, but financial markets can be affected by numerous unpredictable factors. Thus, the predictions these models make should always be used alongside other forms of analysis.

The effectiveness of a probabilistic model relies heavily on the quality of the input data. If the historical data used to determine the probabilities is imprecise or incomplete, the model's predictions may be unreliable. Consequently, thorough data collection and cleaning are vital stages in the modeling process. The complexity of probabilistic models can vary widely. Some may only include one or two random variables, while others may integrate dozens. The selection of model complexity depends on the specific task and the available computational resources. Despite their limitations, probabilistic models remain crucial in finance. They provide a structured method to comprehend uncertainty and make quantifiable predictions, helping financial professionals better navigate the intricate and unpredictable world of finance.

In summary, probabilistic models are mathematical frameworks used to estimate the probability of different outcomes in financial markets. They play a key role in risk management, portfolio optimization, derivative pricing, and numerous other financial operations. While these models have their drawbacks, they offer invaluable insights that can guide decision-making in uncertain situations.

To optimize the usefulness of probabilistic models, financial professionals must ensure they use high-quality input data and suitable model complexity. Furthermore, they must remember that these models are just one component of a comprehensive financial analysis strategy. Fundamentally, probabilistic models provide a method to understand and quantify the inherent uncertainty of the financial world. They are a potent tool in the toolkit of any financial professional, facilitating informed decision-making in a volatile marketplace.

Basic Stock Market Terms

Bull Market: A term describing a market scenario where stock prices are rising or predicted to rise. This term, inspired by the charging posture of a bull, signifies investor optimism and positive market sentiment.

Bear Market: Contrarily, a bear market signifies a situation where stock prices are decreasing or anticipated to decrease for an extended period. This market condition embodies investor pessimism and negative market sentiment.

IPO (Initial Public Offering): A process where a private firm becomes public by issuing its initial shares to public investors, typically to raise capital for its operations.

Blue-Chip Stocks: These are stocks of large, established, and financially secure companies with a track record of dependable performance. These stocks are considered safe investments, though they may not yield as high returns as riskier stocks.

Dividend: A share of a company's profits given to shareholders, usually in cash or additional shares. Not all companies distribute dividends, particularly those in their growth stages.

Capital Gain: The profit obtained from selling a security or investment for a price higher than its purchase price. It's a significant portion of the returns for shareholders.

Index: A statistical representation of the fluctuations in a portfolio of stocks that signify a segment of the overall market. Examples include the S&P 500, Dow Jones Industrial Average, and NASDAQ.

Portfolio: A collection of financial investments like stocks, bonds, commodities, cash, and their fund equivalents.

Volatility: The variation degree of a trading price series over time. High volatility implies higher risk and potential returns.

Liquidity: This refers to the ease of buying or selling a specific security in the market without influencing its price. High liquidity signifies a quick transaction with minimal price impact.

Market Capitalization: Also known as market cap, it indicates the total market value of a company's outstanding shares of stock, calculated by multiplying the company's stock price by its total shares outstanding.

P/E Ratio (Price-to-Earnings Ratio): This ratio compares a share's price to its per-share earnings, helping determine if a company's stock price is over or undervalued.

Yield: The income earned from an investment, such as interest or dividends, usually expressed annually as a percentage based on the investment's cost.

Short Selling: A strategy that involves selling borrowed shares, anticipating a drop in share price, thus enabling their repurchase at a lower price for profit.

Broker: An individual or firm that serves as a go-between for an investor and a securities exchange, facilitating securities transactions for clients.

Day Trading: A strategy involving the purchase and sale of securities within the same trading day, aiming to profit from short-term price changes.

Hedge: An investment made to decrease the risk of unfavorable price movements in an asset, typically involving an offsetting position in a related security.

Margin: Borrowing money from a broker to buy stock, enabling the purchase of more stock than one could normally afford.

ETF (Exchange-Traded Fund): A type of security consisting of a collection of securities, such as stocks, often tracking an underlying index.

Bid and Ask: The bid price is the maximum price a buyer is willing to pay for a stock, while the ask price is the minimum price a seller will accept. The difference between these two prices is known as the spread.

Key Stock Market Concepts

Supply and Demand: This is the fundamental law governing the stock market. If the desire to purchase a stock (demand) exceeds the desire to sell it (supply), the price rises. However, if there are more sellers than buyers, the price drops due to an excess in supply.

Price Determination: The cost of a stock is set by the maximum amount someone is willing to pay for it and the minimum amount at which someone is willing to sell it. This negotiation is managed by the stock exchange and constantly changes with market conditions and company news.

Trading Mechanism: Stock trading occurs through stock exchanges like the New York Stock Exchange or NASDAQ. They function as marketplaces for trading stocks and ensure transparency by providing information about prices, volumes, and trends.

Market Orders and Limit Orders: Investors use these two types of orders for buying and selling stocks. A market order is a request to trade a stock at the current market price, whereas a limit order is a request to trade a stock at a specific or better price.

IPOs (Initial Public Offerings): This is the method private companies use to go public by issuing shares to the public. This allows them to raise capital for expansion or other needs. The cost of the new shares is set by the underwriting investment banks.

Secondary Market: After an IPO, company shares are traded in the secondary market where regular investors buy and sell stocks. The company does not profit from these transactions.

Market Indexes: These indicators measure the performance of the overall stock market or a specific market sector. They comprise a group of stocks, such as the S&P 500, which includes 500 of the largest U.S. companies.

Bull and Bear Markets: These terms refer to the general trend and sentiment of the stock market. A bull market is defined by rising prices and optimism, while a bear market is associated with falling prices and pessimism.

Dividends: Some companies distribute a part of their profits to shareholders as dividends. These payments can provide a consistent income for investors and signify a company's financial stability.

Stock Splits: Companies sometimes increase the number of shares available by dividing each existing share into multiple ones. This makes the stock more affordable for average investors, but it does not alter the company's total market value.

Short Selling: Investors use this strategy when they predict a stock's price will drop. They borrow and sell shares, intending to repurchase them at a lower price and profit from the difference.

Margin Trading: In this method, investors borrow money from a broker to purchase stocks. This enables them to buy more shares than they could with their available funds, potentially increasing their gains, but also their losses.

Futures and Options: These derivatives grant investors the right or obligation to trade stocks at a future date and at a specified price. They are used for hedging or speculating on price movements.

Market Makers: These firms are ready to buy or sell stocks at publicly quoted prices, providing liquidity to the market.

Circuit Breakers: Stock exchanges implement these measures to temporarily stop trading during periods of extreme market volatility to prevent panic selling.

Insider Trading: This involves trading a company's shares by individuals who have access to confidential company information. Insider trading is illegal and punishable by law.

Analyst Reports: Financial analysts research public companies and provide recommendations on whether to buy, hold, or sell their stocks. These reports can affect the stock price.

High-Frequency Trading: This form of algorithmic trading involves computers making thousands of trades per second to exploit minor price differences. It is controversial as it can contribute to market volatility.

Dark Pools: These are private trading exchanges or forums, hidden from public view. Usually used by institutional investors, they prevent impacting the market price.

Regulatory Bodies: These are government or non-government organizations that regulate the stock market to safeguard investors, ensure fair markets, and maintain financial stability. They include the U.S. Securities and Exchange Commission and the U.K. Financial Conduct Authority.

Significance of Stock Prices

Stock prices are a fundamental aspect of the stock market and greatly influence the broader economy. They function as an indicator of a company's financial state and the overall market condition. The price of a company's stock can be viewed as the current value of its future cash flows, signifying market expectations about the company's future profits. Fluctuations in stock prices mirror changes in these expectations, affected by both company-specific and macroeconomic elements.

Investors utilize stock prices to guide their decisions on purchasing, retaining, or selling stocks. A company's stock price increase often signals good performance, while a decrease may hint at potential issues. This perception influences investor behavior, which in turn affects the stock's supply and demand, subsequently impacting the stock price.

Stock prices also serve as a signaling tool. Companies often utilize changes in their stock prices to guide strategic decisions. For instance, an ascending stock price may suggest that the company should expand its operations, while a decreasing price could indicate the need for cost-cutting measures.

Furthermore, stock prices are instrumental in corporate governance. They offer a gauge of management performance and can sway managerial decisions. If a stock price remains low consistently, it could result in management change or even a company takeover.

Moreover, stock prices contribute to market efficiency. Efficient markets are characterized by stock prices that accurately reflect all accessible information. In such markets, stock prices swiftly react to new information, ensuring resources are assigned to their most productive uses.

Stock prices also psychologically affect investors. A surge in stock prices makes investors feel wealthier, encouraging more spending and stimulating the economy. On the contrary, a drop in stock prices can lead to reduced consumer spending, possibly instigating a recession.

Stock prices can also influence a company's capital cost. A high stock price allows a company to raise capital more affordably by issuing more shares. However, a low stock price makes raising capital more costly for a company.

Additionally, stock prices can impact a company's capacity to attract and retain staff. Many companies include stock options in their compensation packages. If the company's stock price is high, these options become more appealing, aiding the company in attracting and retaining employees.

Lastly, stock prices significantly affect mergers and acquisitions. The stock price of the acquiring and target companies can shape the deal's terms, including the purchase price and payment method.

In conclusion, the role of stock prices in the stock market is multi-dimensional. They not only mirror market expectations about a company's future performance but also shape a broad range of decisions by investors, companies, and policymakers. Therefore, understanding the factors that govern stock prices and their potential impacts is vital for all market players.

However, it's crucial to note that stock prices aren't the sole indicators of a company's health or the economy's state. They should be evaluated along with other financial indicators and economic data to make informed decisions.

Therefore, the final outcome of stock price movements is a complex mix of various economic, financial, and psychological factors. While they play a crucial role in the stock market and wider economy, their interpretation and implications should be viewed from a comprehensive perspective.

Factors Influencing Stock Prices

Company Profits: This is the most direct factor affecting stock prices. The higher a company's profits, the more likely its stock price will increase.

Economic Factors: Variables such as GDP, unemployment rates, and the consumer price index can influence stock prices. A robust economy often results in increased corporate profits and subsequently, higher stock prices.

Interest Rates: Lower interest rates tend to encourage investors to buy stocks due to the reduced cost of borrowing.

Inflation: High inflation may decrease stock prices by eroding purchasing power and potentially leading to increased interest rates.

Investor Sentiment: The collective attitude of investors can sway stock prices. Bullish investor sentiment can elevate stock prices, whilst bearish sentiment can cause them to fall.

Political Events: Occurrences such as elections, policy changes, geopolitical incidents, and trade wars can all impact stock prices.

Supply and Demand: If the demand to buy a stock exceeds the supply, the price increases. Conversely, if supply surpasses demand, the price decreases.

Currency Value: The strength of a nation's currency can influence its stock prices, making them more appealing to foreign investors if the currency is robust.

Natural Disasters: Disruptive events such as hurricanes, earthquakes, and pandemics can negatively impact economies and subsequently, stock prices.

Corporate Actions: Events like mergers, acquisitions, IPOs, and share buybacks can affect a company's stock price.

Technological Innovations: The introduction of new technologies can impact a company's stock price.

Industry Trends: Changes and trends within an industry can affect the stock prices of companies within that industry.

Regulatory and Legal Changes: Alterations in regulations or legal issues can impact a company's stock price.

Management Changes: Changes in a company's leadership can cause fluctuations in its stock price.

Investor Relations: The quality of a company's relationship with its investors can affect its stock price.

Media Influence: Media coverage, whether positive or negative, can influence investor sentiment and thus, stock prices.

Speculation: Speculators can impact stock prices by creating demand or supply through their trading actions.

Global Events: Worldwide occurrences such as wars and economic crises can influence stock prices.

Dividends: Firms that consistently pay dividends may have higher stock prices as they are perceived as more stable and profitable.

Competition: The performance and strategies of rival companies can impact a firm's stock price.

Unexpected News: Sudden news about a company or its industry can cause swift changes in its stock price.

Part: Traditional Approaches

Fundamental Analysis

Investors and financial analysts have often found it difficult to predict stock prices. One common method for attempting this prediction is fundamental analysis. This involves a thorough assessment of a company's overall health, including its financial statements, market trends, and industry position. The aim is to determine the stock's intrinsic value in order to potentially forecast future price movements.

Fundamental analysis is based on the concept that a company's stock price may not always accurately reflect its real value. By closely examining a company's financial status and industry position, investors can pinpoint stocks that are undervalued or overvalued. This valuation can guide investment decisions and potentially predict future price trends.

The process of fundamental analysis starts with an inspection of the company's financial reports, including balance sheets, income statements, and cash flow statements. These provide valuable information about a company's profitability, solvency, and liquidity, all of which can impact its stock price.

Profitability metrics like earnings per share (EPS), return on equity (ROE), and net profit margin are key indicators of a company's profitability. Higher profitability figures could lead to a rise in stock price, as they suggest the company's capacity to generate better returns for shareholders.

Solvency ratios such as debt-to-equity ratio and interest coverage ratio give insights into a company's financial stability. High solvency ratios could mean a riskier investment, possibly causing a drop in the stock price. Lower solvency ratios, on the other hand, can indicate financial stability, potentially increasing the stock's value.

Liquidity ratios, like the current ratio and quick ratio, show a company's ability to meet short-term obligations. A company with high liquidity ratios is generally seen as financially stable, which could positively impact the stock price.

Fundamental analysis also requires an evaluation of a company's standing within its industry, including an analysis of the competitive landscape, understanding of the company's market share, and assessment of the industry's growth potential.

The level of competition within an industry can greatly influence a company's stock price. A company in a highly competitive industry may struggle to maintain profitability, negatively affecting its stock price. Alternatively, a company with a strong industry position could have higher stock prices.

A company's market share is also a key aspect of fundamental analysis. A company with a large market share, often seen as a market leader, could have higher stock prices. A company with a smaller market share may struggle to generate profits, potentially resulting in lower stock prices.

The industry's growth potential is another vital factor in predicting stock prices. High-growth industries could present profitable opportunities for companies, positively impacting their stock prices. However, industries with limited growth potential may pose challenges, potentially causing a decrease in stock prices.

Finally, fundamental analysis includes examining market trends. This involves studying macroeconomic indicators like inflation rates, interest rates, and GDP growth. These can provide insights into the economy's health, which can affect stock prices.

For example, in times of economic growth, companies are more likely to report increased earnings, leading to higher stock prices. Conversely, during economic downturns, companies may struggle to maintain profitability, potentially causing lower stock prices.

High inflation rates can harm stock prices, as they reduce consumers' purchasing power, leading to decreased demand for products and services. Low inflation rates, on the other hand, can boost stock prices, as they increase consumers' purchasing power, leading to increased demand for products and services.

Interest rates also have a significant impact on stock price prediction. High-interest rates can increase companies' borrowing costs, potentially resulting in decreased profitability and lower stock prices. Conversely, low-interest rates can decrease companies' borrowing costs, potentially leading to increased profitability and higher stock prices.

Technical Analysis

For many years, investors and market analysts have relied on traditional approaches for forecasting stock prices, with technical analysis being one of the favored methods. This approach is based on the premise that a stock's past trading activities and price fluctuations can provide a useful basis for predicting its future performance.

Technical analysis entails examining statistical trends related to trading activities, such as historical data on stock prices and trading volumes. The underlying principle of technical analysis is that price movements are not random but follow discernible patterns that can be exploited for profit.

By analyzing price movement, investors can detect trends, such as rising or falling price trajectories, and gain valuable insights into potential future price movements. For instance, if a stock has been steadily increasing in price over a certain period, an investor might anticipate that this trend will persist and opt to purchase the stock.

Trading volume, another crucial element of technical analysis, is essential in determining price direction. It represents the quantity of shares or contracts traded in a security or a whole market within a specific period. High volume usually indicates heightened investor interest and can herald the onset of a new trend.

Besides price trends and volume, technical analysts also examine various chart patterns to forecast future movements. These might include patterns like 'head and shoulders,' 'double top,' and 'triple bottom,' among others. These patterns can offer hints about potential price reversals or continuations.

Technical analysis also employs various indicators and oscillators, such as moving averages, Relative Strength Index (RSI), and Moving Average Convergence Divergence (MACD). These tools assist in identifying overbought or oversold conditions and can signal potential trend reversals.

However, while technical analysis can be a potent tool, it is not without flaws. It largely depends on historical data, and as the saying goes, "past performance is not indicative of future results." Therefore, it should be used alongside other stock price prediction methods and investment strategies.

For instance, fundamental analysis can supplement technical analysis. While technical analysis primarily focuses on price and volume, fundamental analysis considers economic and financial factors to forecast a stock's future price. These might include company earnings, industry trends, and macroeconomic data. Furthermore, behavioral finance is another field that investors can leverage together with technical analysis. It delves into how investor psychology and emotions can impact financial markets. By understanding how emotions like fear, greed, and others can influence investor behavior, one can gain further insights into market dynamics.

Ultimately, forecasting stock prices is not a precise science. Numerous variables are involved, and even the most advanced models cannot guarantee 100% accuracy. However, by employing techniques such as technical analysis, investors can enhance their chances of making informed predictions that can result in profitable trading decisions.

Quantitative Analysis

Predicting stock prices is a crucial part of investment strategy, and there are many traditional methods for doing so. Quantitative analysis is one of the most reliable of these methods. It uses mathematical and statistical models and research to comprehend and predict the behavior of stock prices.

Quantitative analysis employs various statistical tools and mathematical models to handle large amounts of data associated with a specific stock. This data can vary from a company's financial reports to industry trends, macroeconomic factors, and even worldwide economic indicators. 'Quants,' or quantitative analysts, use this data to create models that can forecast a stock's future price movements.

The fundamental belief behind quantitative analysis is that future performance can be predicted based on past behavior and patterns. By examining historical data, quants strive to find patterns or trends that may reoccur in the future. In terms of predicting stock prices, this can result in practical investment strategies.

A key feature of quantitative analysis is the use of various mathematical models. These range from simple linear regression models to more complex neural networks and machine learning algorithms. Regardless of their complexity, these models all aim to identify the mathematical relationship between various factors and the stock price.

Quantitative analysis also involves meticulous measurement. Every variable used in a model, every parameter estimated, and every prediction made is accurately quantified. This emphasis on measurement allows for a high level of precision in predicting stock prices, and allows analysts to test the accuracy and reliability of their models.

Research is crucial in quantitative analysis. New mathematical models are constantly being developed and tested, and the field is defined by a continuous push for more accurate and reliable prediction methods. Research is also conducted to find new predictive variables and to better understand the complexities of the stock market.

Despite quantitative analysis's complexity, its goal is simple: to make accurate predictions about future stock price movements. The models developed through this method aim to give investors a statistical probability of a stock's future price, aiding them in making more informed investment decisions.

One of the main benefits of quantitative analysis is its objectivity. Unlike qualitative methods, which can be influenced by personal judgments and opinions, quantitative analysis is based on hard data. This data-driven approach can help eliminate bias and provide a more accurate representation of a stock's potential.

However, quantitative analysis does have its drawbacks. The accuracy of the models used heavily depends on the quality and reliability of the input data. Any errors or inconsistencies in the data can significantly affect the model's predictions.

Additionally, while quantitative analysis can identify patterns and trends in historical data, it cannot account for unexpected events or changes in market conditions. Therefore, while it can offer a valuable guide, it should not be the only predictor of future stock prices.

Economic Analysis

Predicting stock prices often requires a thorough economic analysis. For those working in finance, it's essential to understand how the economy's overall health significantly influences stock prices.

Forecasting stock prices starts with a macroeconomic overview, examining indicators like GDP growth rates, inflation rates, unemployment rates, and interest rates. These indicators offer a glimpse of the economy's overall status and a hint at the direction of stock price movements.

For instance, robust GDP growth may indicate thriving businesses, potentially leading to increased corporate earnings and consequently, higher stock prices. Conversely, high inflation or unemployment rates may suggest an ailing economy, which could adversely affect stock prices.

However, the relationship between these economic indicators and stock prices isn't always clear-cut. For example, while low-interest rates are generally beneficial for stock prices, if they're too low, they might signal a weak economy, which could depress stock prices.

Also, economic analysis must consider specific sectors within the economy, as the same economic conditions can affect different sectors differently. Thus, understanding the dynamics within various sectors can aid in predicting specific stock movements.

Economic analysis also involves assessing fiscal and monetary policies, which can significantly impact stock prices. Fiscal policies like changes in tax laws or government spending can affect corporate profits, while monetary policies can influence interest rates and the money supply, both of which have implications for stock prices.

Global economic conditions should also be considered when forecasting stock prices. In our interconnected world, events in one country can impact stock markets globally.

Additionally, economic analysis should consider future expectations. Stock prices reflect not just current economic conditions but also investors' future economic expectations. However, economic analysis, while valuable, isn't infallible. Stocks are influenced by numerous factors, many unpredictable. Hence, economic analysis should be used alongside other methods like technical analysis and fundamental analysis.

Moreover, the stock market isn't always rational or predictable. Investor sentiment and psychological factors can often drive stock prices, regardless of underlying economic conditions.

As finance professionals, understanding the limitations of economic analysis is crucial. While it can offer valuable insights, it cannot accurately predict future stock prices and is just one tool among many for a shrewd investor.

In essence, economic analysis is vital in predicting stock prices, involving both a macroeconomic overview and understanding specific sector dynamics. By vigilantly observing economic indicators, fiscal and monetary policies, and global economic conditions, investors can better understand factors that impact stock prices.

However, economic analysis isn't a standalone method and should be combined with other strategies for more accurate predictions. It's also essential to remember that the stock market is influenced by numerous unpredictable factors, so while economic analysis can guide investment decisions, it shouldn't be relied upon exclusively.

Despite its limitations, economic analysis remains a key component of stock price prediction and forms a solid foundation for investors' strategies.

As finance professionals, it's our duty to effectively leverage these tools to make informed investment decisions, aiding our clients in navigating the complex world of stock investing and reaching their financial goals.

Sentiment Analysis

Predicting stock prices is a challenging task that involves various techniques and methodologies, one of which is sentiment analysis. This method, also known as opinion mining, has become increasingly popular due to its effectiveness in forecasting stock price trends. It utilizes computational tools to identify the general market sentiment or mood.

Investor sentiment, indicating how investors perceive the overall market health and specific companies, significantly influences stock prices. Positive sentiment usually leads to a rise in stock prices, while negative sentiment often results in a decline. Sentiment analysis offers a way to gauge this investor sentiment, aiding analysts in predicting future price trends.

The sentiment analysis process involves gathering and examining large quantities of data from diverse sources like news stories, social media posts, and financial reports. This data offers rich insights into the market's mood and can be instrumental in predicting stock prices.

Sentiment analysis employs natural language processing, text analysis, and computational linguistics to identify and extract subjective information from primary sources. This helps analysts determine whether the market sentiment for a specific stock is positive, negative, or neutral.

The strength of sentiment analysis lies in its capacity to collate the overall mood of investors, which can act as an early indicator, signaling potential stock price shifts before they happen. For instance, if sentiment analysis identifies an increasing negative sentiment towards a company due to a recent scandal, this could lead to a decline in the company's stock price, presenting a potential investment opportunity for responsive investors.

However, sentiment analysis isn't foolproof. It's merely one of many tools that investors and analysts can leverage to forecast stock price trends and should be utilized alongside other analytical techniques like fundamental and technical analysis. Fundamental analysis assesses a company's financial health, industry standing, and market competition, while technical analysis examines statistical trends based on historical trading activity. Sentiment analysis can augment these traditional methods by offering additional insights into market mood and investor sentiment.

It's also worth noting that sentiment analysis can be prone to interpretation and bias. For example, different investors might interpret the same news differently, resulting in varied sentiment scores. This underlines the importance of using a robust sentiment analysis algorithm that can accurately capture sentiment nuances.

Event-Driven Analysis

Predicting stock prices is an intricate process that involves various approaches and methods. Among these methods, one of the most effective and commonly used is event-driven analysis. This method involves forecasting stock price movements based on forthcoming events, such as product launches, mergers and acquisitions, earnings reports, and other significant corporate happenings.

Event-driven analysis is a strategy that focuses on how specific events can potentially affect the value of a company's stock. This approach relies heavily on the premise that significant corporate events can be capable of causing substantial shifts in a company's stock price. The magnitude and direction of the change depend on the nature of the event and the market's perception of its impact on the company's future profitability.

For instance, a product launch can serve as a significant event that may impact a company's stock price. If the market perceives the new product as a potential game-changer, it could lead to an increase in the company's stock price. However, if the product fails to meet market expectations, it could result in a decline in the stock's value.

Similarly, mergers and acquisitions (M&A) are significant events that can have a profound impact on a company's stock price. The market tends to react positively to M&A announcements if the deal is expected to create synergies, leading to increased profitability for the combined entity. On the other hand, if the market perceives the deal as overpriced or unlikely to generate expected synergies, the stock price of the acquiring company may decline.

Earnings reports are another crucial event that can influence a company's stock price. These reports provide insights into a company's financial health, profitability, and future prospects. Positive earnings surprises often lead to a rise in the stock price, while negative earnings surprises can lead to a decline.

Further, changes in economic indicators, such as interest rates, inflation rates, and employment data, can also affect stock prices. For instance, an increase in interest rates can lead to a decrease in stock prices as it increases the cost of borrowing, thereby affecting the company's profitability.

Another critical event that can impact stock prices is regulatory changes. If a company operates in a heavily regulated industry, any changes to the regulations can significantly impact the company's operations, profitability, and ultimately, its stock price.

It's also important to note that event-driven analysis is not limited to positive events. Negative events, such as product recalls, lawsuits, or negative publicity, can also significantly impact a company's stock price.

In conclusion, event-driven analysis is a powerful tool for predicting stock prices. However, it requires a deep understanding of the company, industry, and market dynamics. Additionally, it should be used in conjunction with other stock prediction methods to increase the accuracy of the forecast.

While event-driven analysis can provide valuable insights, it's equally vital to consider the overall market sentiment and macroeconomic factors. These elements can also significantly influence stock prices and should be factored into any comprehensive stock price prediction strategy.

Finally, it should be noted that while event-driven analysis can be highly effective, it is also subject to limitations and potential inaccuracies. Unexpected events can occur, and market reactions can be unpredictable. Therefore, it's essential to use this approach as part of a broader, more diversified investment strategy.

Time Series Analysis

Forecasting stock prices has always been a difficult task for investors and financial analysts. A traditional technique frequently used for this is Time Series Analysis. This technique is based on the belief that past patterns will continue in the future, and thus, can be used to predict future stock prices.

Time Series Analysis is a statistical process that uses data points collected over time to identify patterns and trends. Each data point in the series represents the stock price at a specific time. The objective of this method is to use these historical data points to project future prices.

This technique differs fundamentally from cross-sectional analysis, which compares different entities at the same point in time. On the other hand, Time Series Analysis focuses on the changes of a single variable over multiple time points. This method is especially useful for predicting stock prices because stock prices are essentially a function of time and are affected by numerous factors that change over time.

One of the key benefits of using Time Series Analysis is its capability to model a wide range of time-based structures. By capturing seasonality, trends, and irregular cycles in the data, it provides a comprehensive understanding of the underlying patterns influencing stock price movements.

Time Series Analysis consists of various stages. The first stage is identification, where the analyst examines the data to identify potential models based on the observed patterns. The next stage is estimation, where the parameters of the selected models are estimated.

Next, the accuracy of the model is verified in the diagnostic checking stage. If the model fits the data well, it can be used for forecasting. If not, the model may need to be adjusted or a different model selected. The final stage is forecasting, where the fitted model is used to predict future stock prices.

The Auto Regressive Integrated Moving Average (ARIMA) model is often used in Time Series Analysis. It is a flexible tool that can capture a range of standard temporal structures in time series data.

The GARCH (Generalized Autoregressive Conditional Heteroskedasticity) model is another commonly used model, which allows the model's parameters to change over time. It is particularly useful for predicting stock prices as it can account for periods of high and low volatility.

However, it's important to note that while Time Series Analysis can be an effective tool for predicting stock prices, it does have limitations. A significant limitation is its assumption that the underlying processes generating the time series data remain constant over time. This assumption may not always be accurate, particularly in the rapidly changing stock market environment. Furthermore, Time Series Analysis can only identify correlations in the data, not causation. Therefore, it is crucial to complement Time Series Analysis with other methods that can provide insights into the causal relationships influencing stock price movements.

Machine Learning Algorithms

The prediction of stock prices has been a long-standing interest for investors, traders, and financial analysts. However, traditional methods such as fundamental and technical analysis often fall short due to the ever-changing and highly unpredictable nature of the stock market. ML employs predictive models and algorithms to analyze historical data and provide future stock price predictions.

Machine Learning algorithms have the capability to understand from past stock price data and utilise this learned knowledge to forecast future prices. This is achieved by finding patterns and relationships in the data set, which are subsequently used to create a predictive model capable of forecasting future stock prices with a certain degree of precision.

The application of Machine Learning in predicting stock prices involves a two-step process known as training and testing. The algorithm is fed historical data during the training phase, from which it identifies patterns and relationships among various variables. The algorithm's predictive model, constructed during the testing phase, is then used to predict future stock prices, with the accuracy of these predictions subsequently assessed.

Machine Learning algorithms employed for predicting stock prices fall into two categories: supervised and unsupervised learning. Supervised learning involves training the algorithm on a labeled data set, i.e., a data set where the outcome variable, in this case, the future stock price, is known. On the other hand, unsupervised learning involves training the algorithm on an unlabeled data set, where the outcome variable is unknown.

Commonly used Machine Learning algorithms for predicting stock prices include Linear Regression, Decision Trees, Random Forests, and Support Vector Machines. Each has its own pros and cons, and their performance can vary depending on the specific characteristics of the data set.

For example, Linear Regression assumes a linear connection between the input variables and the outcome variable. While it's simple and straightforward to interpret, it might not perform well if the actual relationship is non-linear. Decision Trees can model non-linear relationships but they can overfit the data, meaning they can perform well on the training data but poorly on new, unseen data.

Random Forests are an improvement of Decision Trees, being more robust and less likely to overfit, although they can be computationally demanding. Support Vector Machines are another robust Machine Learning algorithm capable of modelling both linear and non-linear relationships and handling high-dimensional data. However, their performance can be delicate to the selection of tuning parameters and the kernel function. Despite the potential of Machine Learning in predicting stock prices, it's crucial to remember that these algorithms are not foolproof. They rely on mathematical models and assumptions, and their predictions are subject to various sources of error. For example, the quality and relevance of the input data can critically affect the predictions. If the data is noisy, incomplete, or irrelevant, the predictions could be faulty.

Additionally, Machine Learning algorithms can only identify patterns that have already happened. They cannot anticipate unforeseen events or sudden market shifts. Hence, while they can be a helpful tool for predicting stock prices, they should be used in combination with other methods and not as a standalone solution.

News-Based Analysis

Predicting stock prices has long fascinated both financial experts and investors. One conventional method utilized for this purpose is News-Based Analysis. This method involves scrutinizing news events and determining their impact on stock prices. This is not an easy task as it requires a thorough understanding of financial markets and the ability to correctly interpret news events.

News-based analysis falls under the category of fundamental analysis, focusing on external events and news announcements that can sway investor sentiment and, consequently, the direction of stock prices. This may encompass political events, economic indicators, corporate earnings reports, and significant company leadership changes.

The fundamental premise of news-based analysis is that public information has a profound effect on stock prices. Therefore, any significant news events can alter investor sentiment, leading to an increase or decrease in the demand for a specific stock, and subsequently, impacting its price.

Positive news such as robust quarterly earnings, the introduction of a new product, or a favorable change in the regulatory environment can lead to an uptick in a company's stock price.

Conversely, negative news such as disappointing earnings, lawsuits, or adverse government policy can result in a stock price decline.

It's worth mentioning that the effect of news on stock prices isn't always instant. The market may take some time to digest the news, with effects becoming noticeable over days, weeks, or even months. This lag can provide an opportunity for investors to make strategic investment decisions.

Additionally, the impact of news on stock prices can also be swayed by overall market sentiment. In a bullish market, even slightly positive news can lead to a significant price increase. Conversely, in a bearish market, even substantial positive news may not boost the stock price.

News-based analysis necessitates a meticulous approach. It's not just about identifying news events, but also understanding their potential effect on a company's financials. This may entail a deep investigation into the company's financial statements, industry trends, and competitive landscape.

A primary challenge in news-based analysis is distinguishing genuine, impactful news from a sea of news and rumors.

However, relying on trustworthy news sources and corroborating the information can aid in accurate news-based analysis.

Moreover, news interpretation is vital. What may initially seem like positive news could potentially have negative implications, and vice versa. Therefore, it's critical to analyze the news from various angles and consider its long-term implications on the company's performance.

Understanding market psychology is also required in news-based analysis. The market's reaction to news is often influenced more by investor sentiment than the actual impact of the news on the company's fundamentals. Therefore, understanding how the market is likely to perceive and react to the news can be as important as the news itself.

Despite its challenges, when correctly used, news-based analysis can be a potent tool for predicting stock prices. It can provide investors with valuable insights into potential investment opportunities and risks, enabling them to make well-informed investment decisions.

Candlestick Charting

The prediction of stock prices is a vital component of investing and trading. Over time, finance professionals have devised a number of techniques to anticipate future stock values. One traditional method used is Candlestick Charting, a visual depiction of price fluctuations over a set timeframe. Originating in Japan over three centuries ago, it continues to be widely used by global traders and investors.

Candlestick charting is particularly useful as it visually presents the opening, closing, highest, and lowest prices of a stock during a specified period. This visualization helps investors spot market patterns and trends that might not be easily discernible in raw numerical data. It also assists in understanding the psychology and behavior of the market.

In a typical candlestick chart, individual "candles" represent specific time periods. The candle's body shows the opening and closing prices, while the wick or shadow signifies the high and low prices in that period. A filled or colored candle implies the closing price was less than the opening price, indicating a price drop. Conversely, an empty or differently colored candle suggests the closing price was higher, representing a price rise.

The power of candlestick charting lies not just in understanding individual candles but also in recognizing various candlestick patterns. Formed by the positioning of one or more candles, these patterns can suggest potential price reversals or continuations - vital information for traders planning their entry and exit strategies.

Patterns such as Bullish Engulfing, Bearish Engulfing, Hammer, Hanging Man, Doji, and many others each have unique interpretations and implications for potential price movements. They provide traders with signals for making trading decisions. For example, a Bullish Engulfing pattern is viewed as a signal of potential price rise, indicating buyers overpowering sellers. A Bearish Engulfing pattern, however, suggests a potential price drop, signaling sellers are controlling the market.

Nevertheless, candlestick charting, like any other technique, has its drawbacks. While it can offer valuable insights into potential future price movements, it is not foolproof. Market conditions are affected by various elements, including economic indicators, news events, and market sentiment, which are not accounted for in candlestick patterns.

Thus, while candlestick charting is a potent tool for traders, it should not be the only one used. It is most effective when combined with other technical analysis tools, such as trend lines, moving averages, and technical indicators. This combination can confirm the signals given by candlestick patterns and enhance prediction accuracy.

The Moving Average Convergence Divergence (MACD)

The Moving Average Convergence Divergence (MACD) is a well-known momentum indicator in the financial markets that follows the trend. It is used worldwide by traders as a potent tool for technical analysis to forecast price trends and produce buying and selling signals. The main goal of the MACD is to show the connection between two different moving averages of a security's price.

The calculation of the MACD indicator involves subtracting the 26-period Exponential Moving Average (EMA) from the 12-period EMA, resulting in the creation of the MACD line. A 9-day EMA of the MACD line, known as the signal line, is then plotted on top of the MACD line to act as a trigger for buying and selling signals.

The MACD indicator is used in charting to visually represent changes in momentum and trend direction. When the MACD line crosses above the signal line, a bullish signal is produced, indicating a possible optimal time to buy. On the contrary, a bearish signal is generated when the MACD line crosses below the signal line, suggesting it may be the perfect time to sell.

A zero line is also included in the MACD chart, representing the point where the 12-period EMA and 26-period EMA intersect. When the MACD line crosses above the zero line, this shows that the 12-period EMA is higher than the 26-period EMA, indicating upward momentum and a potential buying opportunity. Conversely, when the MACD line crosses below the zero line, this shows that the 12-period EMA is lower than the 26-period EMA, indicating downward momentum and a potential selling opportunity.

The MACD indicator can also identify possible price reversals through divergence. Bullish divergence occurs when the security's price is making new lows while the MACD line is not, suggesting a potential price reversal to the upside. On the other hand, bearish divergence occurs when the security's price is making new highs while the MACD line is not, suggesting a potential price reversal to the downside.

Traders often use the MACD alongside other technical indicators to confirm signals and avoid incorrect breakouts. For example, a trader might use a relative strength index (RSI) or a stochastic oscillator with the MACD to confirm a bullish or bearish signal. However, it's worth noting that the MACD, although powerful, is not perfect. It can sometimes give false signals and is not suitable for use in volatile markets with unclear price trends. Thus, it's crucial for traders to be aware of the MACD's limitations and to use it with other technical analysis tools and strategies.

The Relative Strength Index (RSI)

The Relative Strength Index (RSI) is a widely respected momentum indicator used in technical analysis to measure recent price changes. It's an essential tool for evaluating whether a stock is overbought or oversold. It's a vital aspect of any serious investor's toolkit, offering important insights into market trends and potential reversals.

The RSI method was devised by J. Welles Wilder Jr. and unveiled in his influential 1978 book, "New Concepts in Technical Trading Systems." It is now a commonly used indicator and a standard for traders who depend on technical analysis for their investment decisions.

The RSI is calculated on the average gains and losses over a set period, usually 14 periods. The index fluctuates between 0 and 100, with high and low levels signifying overbought and oversold conditions, respectively. Generally, an RSI over 70 suggests an overbought condition, indicating that a price correction could be near. On the other hand, an RSI below 30 signifies an oversold condition, hinting that the price could bounce back soon.

Investors use the RSI to pinpoint potential entry and exit points. When the RSI crosses above the 30 line, it might be a suitable time to buy, as the stock may be leaving the oversold zone. Similarly, when the RSI crosses below the 70 line, it might be a suitable time to sell, as the stock could be entering the overbought zone.

The RSI isn't only a standalone indicator but also works effectively when paired with other technical analysis tools. For example, investors often pair RSI with pattern recognition tools, searching for divergence between price and RSI trends as this could signify a looming trend reversal.

Additionally, the RSI can also be used to identify a stock's general trend. An RSI above 50 typically indicates a bullish trend, while an RSI below 50 suggests a bearish trend. This can help investors discern the overall market sentiment and tweak their strategies accordingly.

However, like all technical indicators, the RSI isn't infallible. It's known to generate false signals, particularly in turbulent markets.

Therefore, it's always recommended to use the RSI alongside other trading indicators and strategies, instead of solely relying on it.

The RSI also tends to linger in overbought or oversold zones for extended periods during strong uptrends or downtrends. Hence, traders shouldn't depend entirely on the traditional 70 and 30 levels to form trading decisions, as it could lead to missed opportunities or false signals.

Moreover, while the RSI is a potent tool, it's most effective in markets with consistent volatility and trading volumes. In less liquid markets, the RSI may not yield reliable signals. Therefore, it's essential for investors to comprehend the underlying market conditions before using this indicator.

Despite these constraints, the RSI continues to be one of the most popular and extensively used tools in technical analysis. Its capability to identify potential overbought and oversold conditions, along with trend identification, make it a crucial tool in an investor's toolkit.

The Auto-Regressive Integrated Moving Average (ARIMA)

The Auto-Regressive Integrated Moving Average (ARIMA) model is a recognized methodology in predicting stock prices by explaining a specific time series based on its past values. This statistical model aids in comprehending the complexities of time series data and subsequently predicting future data points.

The ARIMA model combines two elements - the auto-regressive (AR) and moving average (MA) models. The AR component involves regression of the variable of interest on its past values, while the MA part models the error term as a linear combination of error terms occurring simultaneously and at different past times.

The integrated component of the ARIMA model, represented by 'd', indicates the order of difference or the number of times the time series is differenced to attain stationarity. A stationary time series has properties that do not vary based on the time it is observed.

One of the strengths of the ARIMA model is its adaptability to represent various types of time series data, including those showing trends, making it a valuable tool for financial analysts and economists in predicting stock prices.

Before employing the ARIMA model, it's crucial to ensure that your time series data is stationary, commonly tested using the Augmented Dickey-Fuller test. If not stationary, the data needs to be transformed.

The model parameters, often denoted as (p,d,q), are then estimated using maximum likelihood estimation, where 'p' is the order of the auto-regressive part, 'd' is the order of differencing, and the 'q' represents the order of the moving average part.

Choosing the correct model parameters is vital as it affects the accuracy of the predictions. Techniques for this include the Akaike Information Criterion (AIC) and the Bayesian Information Criterion (BIC).

Once the parameters are selected and the model is fitted to the data, the ARIMA model can be used for forecasting, providing a point forecast and an interval estimate for the forecast.

The model's accuracy can be evaluated by inspecting the properties of the residuals. The residuals should be uncorrelated and normally distributed with zero mean.

Despite being widely used, the ARIMA model has some limitations. It assumes that the time series structure doesn't change over time, which may not be the case in financial markets where structural breaks are common. It also struggles with sudden market changes or 'shocks', high volatility data, or data following a non-linear pattern.

Nevertheless, the ARIMA model is a potent tool for time series analysis and forecasting, extensively used in finance, economics, and other fields. Its usefulness lies in its capacity to model and predict complex and seemingly random time series data, making it a crucial tool for financial professionals.

Limitations of Traditional Prediction Techniques

A significant disadvantage of conventional prediction techniques is their reliance on historical data. They make the assumption that the future will mirror the past, which is not always accurate, especially in the case of financial markets where past performance doesn't always indicate future results. Such assumptions can lead to erroneous predictions that can impact investment strategies.

Traditional prediction methods depend heavily on linear relationships and have difficulty with complex or nonlinear patterns, which can affect the accuracy of predictions in dynamic financial markets. These markets are influenced by a plethora of factors such as geopolitical events, technological advancements, and changes in consumer behavior which can create nonlinear patterns that traditional methods find challenging to comprehend. Conventional prediction models also lack flexibility due to their fixed mathematical structures, preventing them from adapting to changes in the underlying data. Modern predictive models, on the other hand, offer more flexibility and can adjust their structure based on the input data, leading to more accurate predictions. Traditional prediction techniques need large volumes of data for accurate predictions, which can be a significant disadvantage in situations with limited data availability. Collecting, cleaning, and processing such large amounts of data can be time-consuming and expensive.

Another disadvantage is their assumption of normality in the data distribution. Traditional prediction techniques presuppose that data follows a normal or Gaussian distribution, while in reality, financial data often exhibits skewness, kurtosis, or heavy-tailed distributions, which these traditional models fail to account for. These techniques often consider variables separately, disregarding their interactions. However, in real-world situations such as financial markets, variables often influence each other, and disregarding these interactions can lead to inaccurate predictions. Overfitting is another issue with these techniques. This happens when a model is overly complex relative to the number of observations, performing well on training data but poorly on new, unseen data.

Traditional prediction techniques often lack transparency, providing no insight into the variables driving the predictions.

This lack of transparency can make it difficult for decision-makers to understand the logic behind the predictions and trust them. These techniques also struggle with high-dimensional data. In today's data-rich environment, financial analysts often deal with high-dimensional data sets. Traditional methods struggle with the "curse of dimensionality," where the data's volume, complexity, and dimensionality can degrade the model's performance. Building and interpreting traditional prediction models typically require expert knowledge, which can be a significant barrier for organizations without such expertise. Modern machine learning models, however, can automate much of the model selection and tuning process, reducing the need for expert intervention. Traditional methods may also struggle with incomplete or missing data, as they often require complete datasets to function correctly.

They are also less effective at predicting rare events, such as financial crises or market crashes. These techniques are typically static, offering a snapshot prediction at a specific point in time and are less effective at handling the dynamism of financial markets. Traditional prediction techniques often assume that the variables are stationary, meaning their mean and variance do not change over time. However, many financial time series, such as stock prices or exchange rates, are non-stationary, which can lead to inaccurate predictions.

These techniques also often struggle with multicollinearity, where two or more predictor variables in a regression model are highly correlated, making it difficult to determine the effect of individual predictors on the response variable.

Traditional prediction techniques can be computationally intensive, especially when dealing with large datasets. This can lead to longer processing times and higher computational costs. They also struggle with heteroskedasticity, which can lead to inefficient and biased estimates.

Outliers can significantly impact traditional prediction techniques, leading to inaccurate predictions. These methods also require assumptions about the underlying data and relationships between variables, and if violated, can lead to biased or inefficient estimates.

Lastly, traditional prediction techniques often fail to capture the full complexity of financial markets, struggling to incorporate all the factors that influence financial markets, such as macroeconomic trends to investor psychology, thus limiting their predictive accuracy.

Part: Understanding the World of Probability-Based Models

Probabilistic Models

Probabilistic models are statistical tools widely used in various fields, including finance, to forecast the likelihood of different outcomes. These mathematical models are built on a series of assumptions related to the data generating process and apply principles from probability theory and statistics. In the financial sector, these models aid in risk assessment, investment decision-making and derivatives pricing.

These models are crucial for financial analysts and investors as they make it possible to consider multiple potential outcomes and their respective probabilities. This aids in making more informed decisions. These models account for elements of randomness and uncertainty, reflecting the unpredictable nature of financial markets.

Construction of these models involves employing probability distributions, mathematical functions that provide the probabilities of occurrence of various potential outcomes. There are several types of probability distributions like normal, binomial, and Poisson distributions, each suitable for different types of data and situations.

Creating a probabilistic model requires defining the variables to be included in the model and their relationships. For example, in finance, the variables could be asset prices, interest rates, or macroeconomic indicators. These relationships are established by the model's structure, typically represented mathematically.

Assumptions underlying these models are critical and should mirror the characteristics of financial markets and the nature of the investment decisions. Real-world data is then used to estimate the parameters of these models.

In finance, their wide usage in risk management helps firms quantify potential losses under different scenarios. This is especially crucial in portfolio management where balancing expected returns against potential losses is needed.

Probabilistic models also significantly contribute to derivatives pricing. They enable the valuation of complex financial instruments like options and futures, which are dependent on future asset movements. The Black-Scholes model, one of the most renowned probabilistic models in finance, serves this purpose.

Probabilistic models also aid in investment strategy by predicting future performance of different asset classes or individual securities, thus assisting investors in making capital allocation decisions. They are also utilized in financial econometrics, a branch of economics that applies statistical methods to analyze financial data.

However, these models are not without limitations. They are heavily dependent on the assumptions made during their formulation, and if these don't hold, the predictions may not be accurate. Therefore, regular updates and validation using new data are crucial.

Additionally, probabilistic models can be computationally demanding, particularly with large datasets or complex variable relationships, requiring advanced software and hardware. And while they can handle uncertainty to a certain degree, they may struggle to capture the complexities of financial markets fully, such as market crashes or periods of extreme volatility.

Despite these challenges, probabilistic models remain a vital tool in finance due to their ability to quantify and manage risk, price derivatives, and guide investment decisions.

The Role of Probabilistic Models

Probabilistic models are crucial tools in various areas, including finance, where they bring a level of precision and sophistication to prediction and decision-making procedures. They are employed in finance to calculate the risk related to diverse financial tools and portfolios, forecast future prices, and make strategic investment decisions.

A probabilistic model is a mathematical representation of a chance event, defined by a series of probabilities. In finance, these models are helpful in predicting a range of potential results for a specific situation, providing a spectrum of scenarios rather than one, deterministic outcome. This capability to predict various possible outcomes is why these models are especially beneficial in risk management.

Risk management is a vital component of finance, involving the identification, evaluation, and management of potential risks to minimize losses. Probabilistic models can assist in this process by offering a mathematical framework for quantifying risk. For instance, Value at Risk (VaR) is a widely used risk measure that employs probabilistic models to estimate the possible loss an investment portfolio might experience over a certain timeframe under normal market circumstances.

In the intricate world of financial markets, probabilistic models can assist investors and analysts in grasping the probability of different market outcomes. By allocating probabilities to various scenarios, these models can assist decision-makers in assessing the potential risks and rewards of different investment strategies. Furthermore, probabilistic models are also employed in pricing financial derivatives. The Black-Scholes-Merton model, for instance, is a probabilistic model used to compute the theoretical price of options and derivatives. This model presumes that financial markets are efficient and that the prices of financial tools follow a geometric Brownian motion with constant volatility.

Asset pricing is another field where probabilistic models are indispensable. These models assist in determining an asset's intrinsic value, considering various factors like future cash flows, interest rates, and risk factors. By comprehending the probability distribution of future cash flows, investors can make more educated decisions about an asset's fair value.

Probabilistic models are also vital in portfolio optimization. The Modern Portfolio Theory (MPT), a theory that suggests how rational investors should use diversification to optimize their portfolios, heavily relies on probabilistic models. MPT uses these models to estimate the expected returns and variance (or risk) of different portfolio combinations, assisting investors in building portfolios that maximize expected returns for a given risk level. Similarly, probabilistic models are also employed in the field of algorithmic trading. These models can aid traders in predicting price movements and executing trades at the most favorable moments. By analyzing past market data and using probabilistic models to predict future price trends, algorithmic trading systems can generate substantial profits.

In credit risk modeling, probabilistic models are used to estimate the likelihood of a borrower defaulting on a loan. This aids financial institutions in assessing the risk associated with lending and in setting suitable interest rates. Probabilistic models used in credit risk modeling often take into account a variety of factors, including the borrower's credit history, income level, and the overall economic conditions.

Moreover, insurance companies use probabilistic models extensively for underwriting and pricing insurance policies. These models assist insurers in estimating the probability of a claim being filed and the potential size of the claim, allowing them to set premiums that accurately reflect the risk they are taking on.

Different Kinds of Probability Models

The Autoregressive Integrated Moving Average (ARIMA)
The Autoregressive Integrated Moving Average (ARIMA) model is a favored probabilistic tool utilized in forecasting stock prices in the financial sector. It is composed of three elements: autoregression, differencing, and moving average. The ARIMA model leverages past data to predict future values in a time series, making it an effective tool in forecasting future trends.

The Autoregressive (AR) component of the ARIMA model signifies a variable that is dependent on its past values. This suggests that the model uses historical stock prices to predict future prices, which is particularly useful when the stock price trends remain consistent over time.

The Integrated (I) component signifies the differencing of observations to attain stationary time series data. Put simply, this component aids in eliminating trends or cyclical patterns in the data. This is crucial as non-stationary data can produce misleading results and inaccurate forecasts.

The Moving Average (MA) component is a model that analyzes the relationship between an observation and a residual error from a moving average model applied to lagged observations. The aim of the MA component is to comprehend the error of past forecasts to enhance future predictions.

The strength of the ARIMA model is its capability to model a broad spectrum of time series data. It is specifically engineered for non-stationary time series data, making it a good fit for predicting stock prices, which are typically volatile and unpredictable.

One of the key benefits of the ARIMA model is its adaptability. It can manage complex situations as it considers the time-dependent structure of the data. The model can swiftly adjust to abrupt shifts in trends, making it a potent tool in analyzing and forecasting stock market prices.

However, the ARIMA model does have its shortcomings. A key disadvantage is its assumption that the underlying time series data is linear and follows a specific distribution. This may not always be the case in real-world situations as the stock market is influenced by a multitude of factors, many of which are non-linear and do not adhere to a specific distribution.

Another drawback is the ARIMA model's heavy reliance on historical data, implying that it may not be very effective in forecasting stock prices during periods of economic turmoil or drastic changes, where past trends may not accurately predict future outcomes.

Despite these drawbacks, the ARIMA model is still a widely utilized and highly effective tool in financial forecasting. Its capability to handle a broad range of time series data and adapt to changing trends makes it a dependable model for predicting stock prices.

Case Study: Using ARIMA to Forecast Stock Prices

The Autoregressive Integrated Moving Average (ARIMA) model is a well-established technique for time series forecasting, often implemented in financial markets to forecast future values based on historical data. This case study explores its use in predicting stock prices.

The case study focuses on a leading tech company listed on the NYSE. The objective is to use the ARIMA model to forecast the company's future stock prices. The study begins with historical stock price data covering a five-year period, which is then divided into training and testing datasets.

The ARIMA model is identified by three main parameters: p (autoregressive lags), d (order of differencing), and q (moving average). In this context, the model is identified by analyzing the autocorrelation and partial autocorrelation plots of the time series data.

The model fitting process includes maximizing the likelihood function. The ARIMA model is fitted to the training dataset by estimating the parameters that maximize the likelihood of the data. Once the model parameters are estimated, the model can predict future stock prices.

The ARIMA model's forecasts are based on the assumption that the future values of the time series are a linear function of its past values and error terms. The model presumes the time series to be stationary, meaning its properties do not depend on the time the series is observed.

The model's proficiency is measured by its ability to accurately predict the testing dataset. The predictions are compared with the actual stock prices in the testing dataset using various accuracy measures like the Mean Absolute Percentage Error (MAPE), Root Mean Squared Error (RMSE), and the Mean Absolute Error (MAE).

In this case study, the ARIMA model showed a notable degree of accuracy in forecasting the tech company's stock prices, with its ability to account for trends and seasonality in the data contributing greatly to this accuracy.

However, despite the ARIMA model's proven proficiency in forecasting, it's crucial to remember that stock prices are affected by numerous factors, many of which cannot be captured in a time series model. Market sentiment, economic indicators, and geopolitical events can significantly impact stock prices, and these are not captured in historical stock price data.

Furthermore, the ARIMA model assumes that the underlying process generating the time series data remains constant over time. This assumption can be violated in the stock market, where structural shifts and market changes are typical.

While the ARIMA model showed a considerable degree of success in forecasting the tech company's stock prices, the probability of successful stock price estimation can vary greatly depending on the characteristics of the individual stock and the overall market conditions.

Scenario:

Imagine you're a financial analyst at an investment firm, managing a portfolio containing shares from a prominent tech firm, Company X. To make knowledgeable investment decisions, you need to project the future stock prices of Company X.

Strategy:

Compile Past Data: Accumulate five years' worth of Company X's historical stock price data.

Separate Data: Segment this data into a training set (70% of the data) and a testing set (the remaining 30%).

Determine ARIMA Model Parameters: Examine the autocorrelation and partial autocorrelation plots of the time series data to identify the parameters (p, d, q) for the ARIMA model.

Calibrate the Model: Use the training dataset to calibrate the ARIMA model by determining the parameters that maximize the data's likelihood.

Forecast: Utilize the calibrated model to predict future stock prices.

Evaluate Accuracy: Contrast the model's predictions with the actual stock prices in the testing dataset using accuracy measures like MAPE, RMSE, and MAE.

Improve the Model: Based on the model's accuracy, tweak the parameters and recalibrate the model as needed.

Consider Other Factors: Remember that the ARIMA model doesn't account for external factors such as market sentiment, economic indicators, and geopolitical events. Thus, reinforce your ARIMA model forecast with qualitative analysis from these areas. Make Investment Decisions: Use the projected prices, along with other pertinent information, to make knowledgeable decisions about purchasing, trading, or retaining Company X's stocks.

In real-world situations, the ARIMA model can serve as a guide for investment decisions, but it shouldn't be the sole resource. It's crucial to combine this with other forecasting methods and qualitative market analysis to make optimal investment decisions.

Generalized Autoregressive Conditional Heteroskedasticity (GARCH)

Financial analysts, traders, and portfolio managers rely heavily on probabilistic models to forecast future market trends, price variations, and stock market volatility. One such popular model is the Generalized Autoregressive Conditional Heteroskedasticity (GARCH) model. Its main application is in predicting the volatility of returns for diverse financial instruments, such as stocks, bonds, and market indices. Understanding and forecasting volatility, which refers to the fluctuation in a financial instrument's trading price over a specific period, is vital for managing risk in financial markets.

The GARCH model is an extension of the Autoregressive Conditional Heteroskedasticity (ARCH) model, which was created by economist Robert F. Engle. The GARCH model incorporates lagged values of the forecast variance into the equation. It's particularly effective with financial time series data, which often show periods of varying volatility.

One of the GARCH model's primary advantages is its ability to model and predict changing volatility, capturing 'volatility clustering' often seen in financial markets. This pattern, where periods of high volatility are often followed by similar periods, and likewise for periods of low volatility, is especially useful for options pricing, risk management, and financial derivatives. Additionally, the GARCH model can handle other complexities in financial data, such as leptokurtosis and skewness. Leptokurtosis refers to the distribution's heavy-tailed or outlier nature, indicating a higher likelihood of extreme events than in a normal distribution. Skewness refers to the asymmetry of a real-world random variable's probability distribution around its mean.

In finance, the GARCH model is a highly respected tool for forecasting future volatility. It's often employed in risk management, portfolio optimization, and options pricing. Through its ability to model changing volatility, it aids traders and portfolio managers in making more informed decisions.

The GARCH model has been adapted and enhanced in various ways to more accurately represent financial data. For example, the Integrated GARCH (IGARCH) model suggests that conditional variance shocks are persistent over time, a feature frequently seen in financial data. The Exponential GARCH (EGARCH) model allows for asymmetries in the volatility response to shocks, capturing the 'leverage effect' seen in stock returns. However, the GARCH model is not without its flaws. A significant criticism is its assumption that past returns drive volatility. Critics argue this oversimplifies the situation and overlooks other potential volatility influencers, such as macroeconomic news or market sentiment shifts.

Case Study: Foreseeing Stock Prices with GARCH Model

As an expert finance writer, I've always been fascinated by different models used to predict stock prices. One of these models is the Generalized Autoregressive Conditional Heteroskedasticity (GARCH) model which plays a crucial role in analyzing and predicting future shifts in stock prices. To demonstrate, let's examine a hypothetical scenario with a company named 'ABC Corp'.

ABC Corp, a blue-chip company, is listed on NASDAQ. In recent months, the company's stock prices have shown considerable variations. To predict these prices and comprehend the volatility, we will apply the GARCH model.

The GARCH model is a statistical model that uses historical data to predict future variances. Basically, it presumes that a financial instrument's volatility is not consistent but is influenced by past errors and variances. This model is particularly useful in volatile financial markets, such as ABC Corp's case.

To begin, we will gather ABC Corp's past stock prices and feed them into the GARCH model. The model will analyze the data, taking into account previous errors (unexpected changes in stock prices) and variances (the square of previous errors). The model then uses this data to estimate future stock price volatility.

The GARCH model's effectiveness is in its ability to account for volatility clustering, a common occurrence in financial markets. It's observed that days of high volatility tend to be followed by similar days, and the same applies to low volatility days. The GARCH model successfully captures this characteristic, making it a valuable tool for our study.

From applying the GARCH model, we find it efficiently captures the volatility in ABC Corp's stock prices. The model indicates high volatility during product launches and low volatility during stable operational periods. It also predicts increased volatility in the future due to the company's ambitious expansion plans.

One major advantage of the GARCH model is its ability to measure the uncertainty or risk linked with the prediction. This is highly valuable for risk management. With the model's results, investors can assess the risk of investing in ABC Corp and adjust their investment strategies accordingly.

In terms of application, the GARCH model offers dynamic insights for various stakeholders. For financial analysts, the model's results are crucial for pricing derivatives, portfolio optimization, and risk management. For individual investors, the model's predictions can aid in making informed investment decisions.

However, like all models, GARCH has its limitations. It assumes that large changes in stock prices will be followed by more large changes and small ones by more small changes, but this isn't always true. Also, the model is backward-looking and does not consider future events that could influence stock prices. Despite these limitations, in ABC Corp's case, the GARCH model provided a reasonably accurate prediction of stock price volatility. The model successfully anticipated periods of high and low volatility, in line with the company's operational activities.

Let's contemplate a realistic situation where the GARCH model could be beneficial. Imagine that we're financial analysts at a hedge fund and we're looking at ABC Corp as a potential investment for our portfolio. We need to evaluate the risk involved in this investment due to the recent fluctuations in ABC Corp's stock prices.

To begin, we collect historical stock price data for ABC Corp and feed it into the GARCH model. This model scrutinizes the data, taking into account previous errors and variances, and then predicts future stock price volatility. The model's findings indicate high volatility during product launches and low volatility during stable operational periods. The model also forecasts an uptick in volatility due to the company's impending expansion plans.

To devise a practical strategy, we can use the GARCH model's projections to modify our investment approach. For instance, if the model predicts high volatility during product launches, we may choose to offload some of our ABC Corp stocks before a launch to shield our portfolio from potential losses. On the flip side, if the model predicts low volatility during stable operational periods, we might decide to purchase more ABC Corp stocks during these periods to capitalize on potential profits.

Furthermore, the GARCH model's risk assessment can help us evaluate the total risk of adding ABC Corp to our portfolio. If the model suggests a high risk level, we may opt to assign a smaller portion of our portfolio to ABC Corp or even abstain from investing in the company.

Lastly, we can use the GARCH model's forecasts to guide our hedging tactics. For example, if the model predicts high volatility in the future, we might decide to invest in options contracts to hedge against potential losses.

Let's examine a basic example. Assume that the daily stock returns of ABC Corp are denoted by 'R'. The GARCH model suggests that the variance of 'R' is influenced by its historical values. Thus, the variance of 'R' on day 't' can be expressed as $Var(R_t) = \alpha_0 + \alpha_1 \ast e_{t-1}^2 + \beta_1 \ast Var(R_{t-1})$, where α_0, α_1, and β_1 are parameters that need to be estimated, and e_{t-1} is the error term from a mean equation.

Consider the following ABC Corp's stock returns from the last three days:

Day 1: R_{t-1} = 2% (0.02)

Day 2: R_t = -1% (-0.01)

Day 3: R_{t+1} = ?? (This is the value we aim to predict)

We will also assume specific values for our parameters, which are usually determined by maximum likelihood estimation:

$\alpha_0 = 0.00001$

$\alpha_1 = 0.1$

$\beta_1 = 0.8$

We calculate the variance of the returns on Day 2, $Var(R_t)$, using the equation: $Var(R_t) = \alpha_0 + \alpha_1 \ast e_{t-1}^2 + \beta_1 \ast Var(R_{t-1})$.

Here, $e_{t-1} = R_{t-1} - E(R_{t-1})$. Assuming $E(R_{t-1}) = 0$ (a common assumption for stock returns), we obtain $e_{t-1} = 0.02$. Substituting these values, we get: $Var(R_t) = 0.00001 + 0.1\ast(0.02)2 + 0.8 \times 0.00001 = 0.000014$.

To predict the variance of returns on Day 3, $Var(R_{t+1})$, we use the same equation but with the values from Day 2: $Var(R_{t+1}) = \alpha_0 + \alpha_1 \ast e_t^2 + \beta_1 \ast Var(R_t) = 0.00001 + 0.1\ast(-0.01)2 + 0.8 \times 0.000014 = 0.0000124$.

This variance can be used to predict the returns on Day 3 using a mean equation. For example, if we assume that the mean equation is $R_t = e_t \ast \sqrt{Var(R_t)}$, where e_t is a random variable with zero mean and unit variance, then the projected return on Day 3 would be $R_{t+1} = e_{t+1} \ast \sqrt{0.0000124}$.

Therefore, the GARCH model helps us anticipate the volatility of the stock prices, which can be used to predict the stock return. However, this is a basic example, and real financial forecasting involves much more complexity and uncertainty.

Vector Autoregression (VAR)

In the financial world, probabilistic models, especially for predicting stock market prices, have become indispensable. The Vector Autoregression (VAR) model, in particular, has garnered considerable interest. This piece will explore VAR, its function, and its influence on determining stock prices.

The VAR model, an extension of the univariate autoregressive model, is a multivariate time series model that encapsulates the linear interdependencies among multiple time series. It is particularly adept at modeling the dynamic behavior of economic and financial time series and for forecasting.

The VAR model uses a linear combination of a variable's past values and the past values of all other variables in the system to model the variable's current value. It's a stochastic process that captures the linear interdependencies among multiple time series and allows for the consideration of more than one evolving variable at a time. In econometric analysis, the VAR model is recognized as a crucial tool.

It's important to highlight that in a VAR model, each variable is a linear function of its own past values and the past values of all other variables. This characteristic has made VAR models especially appealing in the finance sector where multiple variables often simultaneously interact.

In relation to the stock market, VAR can be employed to measure the relationships between the prices of different stocks over time. For example, if the prices of stock A and stock B have historically moved together, a VAR model could assist in predicting the future price of stock A based on both stocks' past prices.

Additionally, the VAR model enables the inclusion of lagged values of variables, which is particularly useful in predicting stock prices. This is because stock prices are frequently influenced by their own historical values and the historical values of other pertinent variables.

VAR models can provide insights into how shocks to one variable will affect other variables in the system. Traders and investors can use this information to understand how different stocks might respond to changes in each other's prices, potentially leading to more informed investment decisions.

One of the main benefits of VAR models is their capacity to consider the interrelationships among multiple time series data. In the stock market, where numerous variables can affect a particular stock's price, this can be incredibly beneficial.

However, it's also important to acknowledge that while VAR is a potent tool, it does have its constraints. For example, it presumes linearity and struggles with non-linear relationships. Therefore, it's essential to take these factors into account when using VAR models to predict stock prices.

Moreover, VAR models necessitate vast amounts of data to be effective. This can sometimes be a limiting factor, especially for newer companies or stocks without a comprehensive history of available data.

Despite these limitations, the VAR model continues to be a vital instrument for financial analysts and traders. It facilitates a sophisticated understanding of the intricate factors influencing stock prices and can greatly assist in making reliable forecasts.

Here's a detailed process on how to use VAR to predict stock prices for an investor:

Firstly, identify the variables: The initial step is to pinpoint the variables that could potentially influence the stock prices you're trying to predict. These might include other stock prices, economic indicators like GDP or inflation rates, and even global factors such as oil prices.

Secondly, collect historical data: Once you've identified the variables, gather past data for these variables. The more data you have, the more likely your VAR model will be accurate.

Thirdly, establish the VAR order: The VAR order relates to the number of lagged variable values included in the model. Utilize statistical tests, such as the Akaike Information Criterion (AIC), to ascertain the proper order.

Fourthly, estimate the VAR model: This step involves conducting multiple regression analyses, one for each variable in the model. Each regression comprises the lagged values of all the variables as predictors.

Fifthly, check for stationarity: The VAR model presumes that the variables are stationary, meaning their mean and variance remain constant over time. If this presumption isn't met, you might need to alter your data or difference your variables.

Sixthly, interpret the coefficients: The coefficients in a VAR model indicate the change in the dependent variable associated with a single unit change in the predictor variables. They can assist you in understanding the relationships between the variables.

Seventhly, forecast future values: Once your model is estimated and checked, use it to predict future variable values. This could help you forecast future stock prices.

Eighthly, verify the accuracy of your forecasts: Compare your predicted values with the actual values to verify the accuracy of your forecasts. You can utilize measures like the Mean Absolute Error (MAE) or the Root Mean Squared Error (RMSE) for this.

Ninthly, update the model occasionally: You should update your VAR model as you acquire more data, to maintain its accuracy. This is particularly important in fast-changing markets.

Lastly, use the forecasts to guide your investment decisions: The ultimate purpose of predicting stock prices is to make knowledgeable investment decisions. Use your VAR model's forecasts to inform your investment strategy.

Let's look at a realistic situation where an investor, John, is looking to forecast the stock prices for Company A. He thinks that Company A's stock prices are influenced by the stock prices of Company B and C, GDP growth, and oil prices.

Step 1: Variable Identification - Stock prices of companies B and C, GDP growth, and oil prices are the factors John decides to incorporate in his model.

Step 2: Gather Historical Data - John collects historical data on these variables to enhance the accuracy of his VAR model.

Step 3: Determine the VAR Order - John employs AIC to decide the number of past variable values to include in his model.

Step 4: VAR Model Estimation - John performs multiple regression analyses for each variable, using past values of all the variables as predictors.

Step 5: Test for Stationarity - John ensures the mean and variance of his variables are consistent over time. If not, he modifies his data accordingly.

Step 6: Coefficient Interpretation - John interprets the coefficients in his model to understand the relationships among the variables.

Step 7: Forecast Future Values - John uses his verified model to predict future stock prices for Company A.

Step 8: Confirm Forecast Accuracy - John compares his forecasted values with actual values to assess his forecast's accuracy, using measures like MAE or RMSE.

Step 9: Update Model Periodically - John regularly updates his VAR model with new data to maintain its accuracy as market conditions change.

Step 10: Apply Forecasts to Investment Decisions - John's investment strategy is guided by his VAR model's forecasts, deciding whether to buy, sell, or hold Company A's stocks.

Practical Tactics for Real-Time Situations:

Regular Monitoring: John should regularly observe the variables he identified as affecting Company A's stock prices. For instance, if oil prices show a significant shift, he might need to modify his VAR model.

Incorporate External Factors: John needs to take into account external factors that could influence his variables, such as a sudden political event affecting GDP growth.

Diversify Investments: John should not solely depend on the VAR model's forecasts. Diversifying his investments can help reduce risk.

Let's take a look at a simplified example where John is trying to forecast Company A's stock prices based on the stock prices of Companies B and C. First, he gathers historical stock prices:

Company A's stock prices: $100, $102, $104, $106, $108.

Company B's stock prices: $80, $82, $84, $86, $88.

Company C's stock prices: $90, $92, $94, $96, $98.

We're working under the assumption that Company A's prices are influenced by Companies B and C's prices.

Using this historical data, John creates a VAR model. For simplicity, let's say the model's equation is:

$$A(t) = a + bB(t-1) + cC(t-1)$$

In this equation:

$A(t)$ represents Company A's stock price at time t.

$B(t-1)$ and $C(t-1)$ are the stock prices of Companies B and C at time t-1.

The coefficients we need to calculate are a, b, and c.

To determine these coefficients, we can employ regression analysis. Let's assume that the estimated coefficients are $a=2$, $b=0.3$, and $c=0.4$.

Now, if Companies B and C's stock prices at time t are $B(t)=\$90$ and $C(t)=\$95$ respectively, we can forecast Company A's stock price at time t+1 as: $A(t+1) = 2 + 0.3\times90 + 0.4\times95 = \$71$

John can verify the model's accuracy by comparing the forecasted value with the actual stock price at time t+1 when it becomes available. If the forecasted value is similar to the actual value, the model is accurate. If not, John can modify the model by adjusting the coefficients or adding more variables, such as GDP growth and oil prices.

Multivariate GARCH (MGARCH)

Investing and trading greatly benefit from financial modeling, as it offers a quantitative method to examine and forecast the performance of a specific stock or the overall market. The Multivariate Generalized Autoregressive Conditional Heteroskedasticity model, or MGARCH model, is a widely accepted probabilistic model used to measure stock prices in the stock market.

This multivariate extension of the GARCH model was developed to improve performance in modeling and forecasting high-dimensional time series data. Despite its complexity, the MGARCH model is renowned for its accuracy and efficiency, particularly when working with multiple variables and high-frequency data, both common in stock market data.

The MGARCH model, based on the Generalized Autoregressive Conditional Heteroskedasticity (GARCH) model, considers the volatility of stock prices for a more realistic prediction of future prices. Its 'multivariate' property allows it to handle multiple, interdependent financial time series, like the prices of numerous stocks.

The MGARCH model assumes that market volatility varies over time, which means periods of high volatility are likely followed by similar periods, and the same applies to low volatility periods. This assumption is particularly relevant in the often volatile financial markets.

The MGARCH model overcomes the limitations of the univariate GARCH model, which can only handle a single time series, by managing multiple time series. This makes it more suitable for portfolio management and risk measurement in financial markets, where multiple assets interact.

The model is also effective in capturing the correlations between different financial assets, a critical factor in portfolio management. By accurately capturing these correlations, the MGARCH model provides a more precise measure of portfolio risk.

The MGARCH model's ability to forecast future volatilities is another significant advantage. In financial markets, volatility is a key risk indicator, so predicting volatility is crucial for traders and risk managers. By utilizing the MGARCH model, they can predict future volatilities more accurately, leading to improved risk management and trading strategies.

However, the MGARCH model has its drawbacks. Its computational complexity, necessitating the estimation of multiple parameters, particularly with high-dimensional data, makes it difficult to implement. Also, it assumes that conditional variances and covariances follow a specific structure, which may not always be the case in real-world financial markets, limiting its applicability.

Despite these limitations, the MGARCH model remains a potent tool for modeling and predicting stock prices due to its capacity to handle multiple time series and capture their correlations. This makes it particularly useful in finance, where assets are typically interdependent.

This guide will concentrate on the application of MGARCH for stock price prediction in real-world situations. It's important to initially recognize that MGARCH models are founded on the concept that the variance of error terms (the discrepancy between actual and forecasted values) fluctuates over time. This is especially pertinent to stock prices, which often exhibit periods of intense fluctuation (for instance, during financial crises) and times of low volatility (like during stable economic phases).

For investors who aim to use MGARCH effectively for predicting stock prices, the following steps should be taken:

Data Gathering: Accumulate historical data of the stocks you wish to predict. This data should encompass variables like opening price, closing price, highest price, and lowest price.

Model Choice: Select the most suitable MGARCH model. There are numerous MGARCH models available, including the VECH model, the diagonal VECH model, the BEKK model, and so on. The model selection is contingent on the data's characteristics and the specific needs of the analysis.

Model Estimation: Calculate the parameters of the MGARCH model using an appropriate method, such as the maximum likelihood estimation (MLE) method. This requires solving a series of equations to find parameter values that maximize the probability of the observed data.

Model Verification: Validate the model's adequacy by reviewing the residuals (the differences between actual and predicted values). If a pattern is observed in the residuals, it suggests that the model is insufficient and requires modification.

Forecasting: Once the model is adequately fitted, it can be used to predict future stock prices. The MGARCH model offers a variance forecast of the error terms, which can be utilized to set up confidence intervals for the predictions.

Model Revision: Periodically revise the model to include the latest data. This ensures the model's continued accuracy and reliability.

For example, suppose you're an investor aiming to forecast future stock prices of a specific company, such as Microsoft.

Data Collection: You would start by amassing historical Microsoft stock data. This data should encompass variables like the opening price, closing price, highest price, and lowest price of the stocks over a substantial time frame.

Model Selection: Based on the traits of the collected data, you would then choose the most appropriate MGARCH model. For example, if the data displays high volatility, you might opt for the BEKK model, which allows previous variances and covariances to influence the current variance.

Model Estimation: Subsequently, you would ascertain the parameters of the chosen MGARCH model using a suitable technique. For example, you might employ the maximum likelihood estimation (MLE) method to solve a sequence of equations and determine parameter values that maximize the probability of the observed data.

Model Verification: You would then confirm the model's sufficiency by examining the residuals. If a pattern is observed in the residuals, it implies that the model isn't perfectly capturing the data and needs adjustment.

Forecasting: Once the model is competently fitted and validated, it can be utilized to predict future Microsoft stock prices. The MGARCH model provides a variance forecast of the error terms, which can be used to establish confidence intervals for the predictions.

Model Revision: As new Microsoft stock price data becomes accessible, you would need to update the model to incorporate this most recent data. This ensures the model remains accurate and reliable.

In real-time situations, you can use the predicted stock prices to make informed investment decisions. For example, if the model forecasts a surge in stock prices, you might choose to buy more stocks. On the other hand, if the model predicts a price drop, you might decide to sell. However, bear in mind that every model has its limitations and should not be the only factor in your investment decisions. Always take into account other factors and strategies as well.

Let's simplify this scenario. Imagine you've gathered data for Microsoft's stock price over the past 5 days, with closing prices as follows:

Day 1: $220
Day 2: $230
Day 3: $240
Day 4: $250
Day 5: $240

We'll use a basic moving average (MA) model to estimate the price for Day 6. This model calculates the predicted price as the average of the previous 'n' days. So, using a 3-day MA model, the estimated price for Day 6 is the average of Days 3, 4 and 5. Hence, the projected Price for Day 6 = (Day 3 + Day 4 + Day 5) / 3 = ($240 + $250 + $240) / 3 = $243.33. This is a rudimentary prediction and doesn't account for stock volatility. To consider this, we could employ a MGARCH model. Assuming we've determined the model parameters via MLE, and discovered the error term variance to be 25, we can utilise this to establish a prediction confidence interval. The 95% confidence interval for the Day 6 prediction is calculated as follows:

Lower Limit = Predicted Price - 1.96*(Standard Deviation) = $243.33 - 1.96*(sqrt(25)) = $243.33 - 1.96×5 = $233.33
Upper Limit = Predicted Price + 1.96*(Standard Deviation) = $243.33 + 1.96×5 = $253.33

Thus, we can assert with 95% certainty that the Day 6 price will range between $233.33 and $253.33. Naturally, this is a simplified scenario and actual models would need to consider a multitude of other factors and utilise more data.

Stochastic Volatility (SV) Models

Stochastic Volatility (SV) models are commonly used tools for estimating and forecasting stock market prices. Their purpose is to predict the fluctuation of stock prices, providing key insights into potential price movements. The foundation of SV models rests on the fact that stock price volatility isn't static but changes unpredictably over time. This unpredictable or 'stochastic' aspect of volatility is what these models aim to capture and forecast. The underlying idea of the SV model is to determine a stock's volatility and use it to predict future prices.

One of the main advantages of SV models is their ability to adapt to the changing nature of stock market volatility. Unlike traditional models, which often incorrectly assume that volatility remains the same over time, SV models account for volatility's changeability. They also acknowledge that changes in stock prices can be asymmetric, meaning prices can fall quicker than they rise, or vice versa. This inclusion of asymmetry allows SV models to provide more precise and detailed predictions of stock price movements.

A crucial feature of SV models is their capability to capture the 'leverage effect', a phenomenon where a stock's price decline leads to increased volatility. This is a frequent occurrence in stock markets, and SV models are uniquely prepared to accommodate it. They also account for volatility clustering, a financial term that describes how periods of high volatility are often followed by similarly volatile periods, and vice versa. This pattern, commonly seen in stock markets, can aid in forecasting future price movements.

The flexibility of SV models comes from their adaptability. They can be adjusted to suit specific market conditions or particular stock types, making them a valuable resource for financial analysts and investors. However, the complexity of SV models poses a challenge. Their use requires a degree of statistical and mathematical knowledge that may be a hurdle for some investors. Nevertheless, the potential advantages of using SV models often outweigh these challenges.

SV models' usefulness extends beyond mere stock price forecasting. They can also be employed in option pricing, portfolio management, and risk management, further increasing their importance in the finance sector.

Guide on Using Stochastic Volatility (SV) Models for Stock Price Forecasting

Stochastic Volatility (SV) models are commonly employed in the financial industry for the purpose of forecasting stock prices. They take into account the dynamic and unpredictable behavior of financial markets, where the volatility or degree of variation of a trading price series can change over time. This guide will provide a practical outline on how to make use of SV models for predicting stock prices.

Step 1: Grasp the Fundamentals of Stochastic Volatility Models

It's crucial to first comprehend what Stochastic Volatility (SV) models are. They operate on the assumption that the volatility of a financial instrument is variable, not fixed, and follows a specific stochastic process. SV models encapsulate the inherent randomness and uncertainty found in financial markets, providing a more accurate depiction of stock price fluctuations.

Step 2: Understand the Mathematics Behind SV Models

SV models are typically represented mathematically. It's necessary to get acquainted with mathematical concepts such as stochastic calculus, differential equations, and probability theory. It's also important to grasp the specific mathematical formulation of the SV model you are employing.

Step 3: Select the Appropriate SV Model

There are various types of SV models, each with its unique characteristics and assumptions. Some popular examples include the Heston model, the Hull-White model, and the GARCH model. It's key to select the model that aligns best with your requirements and understanding.

Step 4: Gather and Refine Your Data

The integrity of your data is essential for the precision of your predictions. You need to collate historical stock price data and refine it to eliminate any errors, outliers, or missing values.

Step 5: Adapt Your Model to the Data

Once your data is ready, you can use statistical software to adapt your SV model to the data. This involves determining the parameters of the model that best represent the characteristics of the stock price data.

Step 6: Evaluate Your Model

After adapting your model, it's important to test its predictive accuracy. This might include using a different set of data to forecast stock prices and comparing these forecasts with the actual prices.

Step 7: Analyze the Results

After testing your model, you should analyze the results. This includes understanding what the estimated parameters of your model signify and how they relate to the stock price's volatility.

Step 8: Maintain and Update Your Model

Since financial markets are dynamic, your model should mirror this. You should consistently update your model with fresh data and re-calculate its parameters.

Understanding and utilizing SV models can be a major advantage for investors. These models provide a more accurate and dynamic perspective of stock prices by capturing the inherent randomness and unpredictability of financial markets. This helps in assessing the risk associated with various investments and making more informed decisions.

One key benefit of SV models is their capacity to forecast volatility. Volatility plays a significant role in financial markets, influencing everything from option pricing to risk management. Furthermore, SV models can accommodate phenomena such as volatility clustering, where periods of high volatility usually follow other periods of high volatility, and vice versa. This can be especially beneficial in predicting stock prices during volatile market conditions.

However, it's worth noting that while SV models are potent tools, they are not infallible. The accuracy of their forecasts is dependent on the quality of the data used and the suitability of the chosen model. Additionally, like all models, they are built on certain assumptions, which may not always be accurate.

Practical Case: Predicting Stock Prices for a Technology Company

Suppose you're an investor keen on predicting the share prices for a technology firm (let's call it TechCo). You've chosen the Heston SV model due to its capacity to manage the intricacies of the tech sector's volatility. Here's how you can apply it in a real-life situation:

Step 1: Gather Past Stock Price Information

Initially, you accumulate past stock price information for TechCo from a credible source. This data encompasses the stock's closing prices over the last five years.

Step 2: Polish Your Data

Subsequently, you polish the data by eliminating any mistakes or outliers. You also fill in any gaps using interpolation or other appropriate methods.

Step 3: Tailor the Heston Model to Your Data
Using statistical software, you modify the Heston model to fit
your refined data. This involves identifying the model's
parameters that best depict the characteristics of TechCo's stock
price data.
Step 4: Assess Your Model
To verify the precision of your model, you use a different data set
(for instance, the stock prices for the past six months) to predict
TechCo's share prices. You then juxtapose these forecasts with
the real prices to evaluate the model's precision.
Step 5: Examine the Results
If the model's predictions closely align with the actual prices, it
signifies that the model is performing effectively. You then
analyze the calculated parameters of your model to comprehend
what they imply about TechCo's share price volatility.
Step 6: Revise Your Model
Considering the dynamic nature of the tech sector, you routinely
revise your model with new data to ensure it aligns with any
market changes.
Practical Approaches for Real-Time Use:
Use the model to predict future volatility: If the model indicates
high volatility in the near future, it might be wise to delay
investing in TechCo until the market stabilizes.
Incorporate the volatility predictions when making investment
decisions: If the model anticipates low volatility, it could be a
suitable time to invest, as the share price is projected to be stable.
Modify your investment strategies based on the model's
conclusions: If the model illustrates a trend of escalating volatility,
contemplate diversifying your portfolio to reduce risk.
Bear in mind, while SV models can be highly beneficial, they are
not always entirely accurate. Always take into consideration other
factors and utilize other tools to make informed investment
decisions.
Let's demonstrate a straightforward application of the Heston
Stochastic Volatility (SV) model using some fictitious data.
We'll hypothesize that TechCo's stock price is currently $100 and
we aim to forecast its value after one year. In the Heston model,
five factors shape the volatility process: the speed of mean
reversion (kappa), the long-term average volatility (theta), the
volatility of volatility (sigma), the initial volatility (v0), and the
correlation between the stock price and its volatility (rho).

Let's also hypothesize that these factors have the following values: 2, 0.04, 0.3, 0.04, and -0.7 respectively.

The Heston model utilizes these factors to formulate two stochastic differential equations (SDEs) that represent the stock price process and the volatility process.

Phase 1: Formulate the SDEs

The SDE for the stock price is:

$$dS = rSdt + \sqrt{v}SdW1$$

And the SDE for the volatility is:

$$dv = kappa(theta - v)dt + sigma \sqrt{v}dW2$$

Here, r represents the risk-free rate, S is the stock price, v denotes volatility, and W1 and W2 are two interrelated Wiener processes with rho as their correlation.

Phase 2: Solve the SDEs

Typically, these SDEs are resolved numerically through methods like the Euler-Maruyama or the Milstein method.

Let's say we use the Euler-Maruyama method with a 0.01 time step, implemented in a computer program. The program projects a stock price of $105 after one year.

Phase 3: Verify the model

We now need to authenticate the model by comparing the predicted price with the real price after one year. If the actual price is $104, then our model is fairly precise.

Phase 4: Analyze the results

The projected parameters of the model could be interpreted as follows: a kappa of 2 suggests that volatility reverts to its mean relatively quickly. A theta of 0.04 indicates that the long-term average volatility is 4%. A sigma of 0.3 signifies a high volatility of volatility. A v0 of 0.04 suggests that the initial volatility is 4%. A rho of -0.7 indicates a strong negative correlation between the stock price and its volatility, i.e., as the stock price increases, its volatility tends to decrease.

Phase 5: Refresh the model

We should regularly revise the model with fresh data to ensure its continued precision.

Hidden Markov Models (HMM)

Probabilistic models, including the Hidden Markov Model (HMM), are vital for analyzing financial markets, especially in relation to stock prices. HMM is a statistical model that assumes a system operates as a Markov process with unknown parameters. The term "hidden" refers to the fact that the state sequence affecting observable parameters is not directly visible, but only the output influenced by the state can be seen.

In the context of stock prices, the "hidden" aspect refers to the underlying economic conditions or company-specific factors impacting stock price changes. The assumption is that the market has different states, each characterized by specific statistical characteristics. Each state signifies a specific market condition, such as a bull market, bear market, or a sideways market. These states can be influenced by various hidden factors like economic indicators, geopolitical events or company-specific news.

The transition from one state to another is determined by probabilities, hence the term "probabilistic" in the model's name. These probabilities can be estimated using past data and then used to predict future market states. This feature makes HMMs useful for predicting changes in market trends, helping investors make informed decisions on when to buy or sell stocks.

HMMs operate by using a sequence of observable data to deduce the sequence of hidden states that likely resulted in that data. In the context of the stock market, observable data could be daily returns while the hidden states could symbolize different market conditions.

The effectiveness of HMMs in predicting stock prices lies in their capacity to capture market changes dynamically. HMMs acknowledge that markets change over time and that these changes impact stock prices. By accurately identifying these shifts, HMMs can provide valuable insights into future price movements.

Nevertheless, HMMs have limitations. One main challenge is determining the appropriate number of hidden states. Too many states can make the model overly complex and prone to overfitting, while too few states can oversimplify the actual dynamics of the stock market.

Another potential drawback is HMMs' dependency on the Markov assumption that the future state is dependent only on the current state and not on the sequence of previous states. This simplifies the model, but it may not always be accurate in the stock market where past trends can influence future movements. Despite these challenges, HMMs' adaptability and versatility make them invaluable tools in financial market analysis. With the right parameters and careful interpretation, they can provide a more in-depth understanding of market dynamics and contribute to more precise predictions of stock price movements. In a world where investors are always looking for an advantage, the use of probabilistic models like HMMs can be a game-changer.

Hidden Markov Models (HMM) are versatile tools that can be used in a wide array of areas including speech and handwriting recognition, bioinformatics, and economics. In the realm of financial markets, HMM can be harnessed specifically for predicting stock prices. This guide aims to provide a comprehensive understanding of how to use HMM effectively to predict stock prices.

To begin with, it is crucial to understand the concept of Hidden Markov Models. These are statistical models that calculate the probability of a sequence of observations, while the states producing these observations remain hidden or unknown. In terms of stock market prediction, the observations might be the daily closing prices and the hidden states could correspond to the inherent market conditions.

Understanding the Data: The first stage in utilizing HMM for predicting stock prices involves understanding the data. Stock prices are affected by numerous factors such as company performance, industry trends, economic indicators, political environment, and investor sentiment. Hence, it is vital to collect and analyze pertinent data to make well-informed predictions.

Data Preprocessing: Generally, stock market data is time-series data that needs to be preprocessed before it can be utilized in a model. This could involve cleaning the data, managing missing values, normalizing the data, and transforming it into a format compatible with the HMM.

Model Training: After data preprocessing, the subsequent step is to train the HMM using your data. This involves using an algorithm, such as the Baum-Welch algorithm, to estimate the parameters of the HMM, which includes the initial state probabilities and the transition probabilities between states.

Model Testing: Following the training of the HMM, the next step is to test it on new data. This involves using the model to predict the hidden states for a new sequence of observations and comparing these predictions with the actual states.

Model Evaluation: Various metrics such as accuracy, precision, recall, and F1 score can be used to evaluate the performance of the HMM. Depending on the results, you might need to adjust the model parameters or preprocess the data differently.

Predicting Future Stock Prices: Once the HMM has been trained and tested, it can be utilized to predict future stock prices. This involves using the model to predict the hidden states for a future sequence of observations.

Model Updating: Given the dynamic and ever-changing nature of stock markets, it is crucial to update the HMM periodically with new data to ensure the predictions remain accurate and relevant.

Remember, while HMM can provide a probabilistic framework for predicting stock prices, they are not infallible. Market conditions are influenced by numerous factors and can change rapidly. As such, HMM should be used as one among many tools when making investment decisions.

Investing in the stock market carries a high degree of risk, and comprehensive due diligence is essential before making any investment decision. While HMM can provide valuable insights into the likely future behavior of stock prices, they cannot guarantee a certain outcome. It is always advisable to consult with a financial advisor or investment professional before making any significant investment decisions.

Scenario: An investment firm's financial analyst aims to forecast the stock prices of a specific company, in this case, Apple Inc, over the next ten days.

Step 1: Data Collection and Understanding - The analyst gathers historical data on Apple's stock prices and associated financial indicators. They also examine factors that could influence the stock prices, such as Apple's financial health, industry trends, economic indicators, political climate, and investor sentiment.

Step 2: Data Preprocessing - The analyst cleans the data, handles any missing values, normalizes the data, and converts it into a format compatible with the HMM.

Step 3: Model Training - The analyst trains the HMM using the preprocessed data. This involves using the Baum-Welch algorithm to estimate the HMM parameters, including the initial state probabilities and the transition probabilities between states.

Step 4: Model Testing - The analyst tests the HMM on a separate new data set, contrasting the model's predictions of hidden states (market conditions) with the actual states.

Step 5: Model Evaluation - The analyst assesses the HMM's performance using metrics such as accuracy, precision, recall, and F1 score. Depending on the results, the analyst might modify the model parameters or preprocess the data differently.

Step 6: Predicting Future Stock Prices - Once the HMM is satisfactorily trained and tested, the analyst utilizes it to forecast the hidden states for the upcoming ten days, and from these, the stock prices.

Step 7: Model Updating - Given the stock market's dynamic nature, the analyst ensures to regularly update the HMM with new data to maintain the accuracy and relevance of the predictions.

Strategies for Real-Time Scenario:

Regularly Update the Model: Given the numerous dynamic factors influencing the stock market, it's critical to regularly update the model with fresh data.

Use Multiple Models: Do not rely solely on HMM. Use it in tandem with other machine learning and statistical models for informed decision-making.

Use Various Data Sources: Utilize information from different sources, such as news feeds, social media, and financial reports, for more accurate predictions.

Monitor Model Performance: Closely monitor the model's performance. Retraining or tweaking the model may be necessary if the accuracy decreases.

Risk Management: Remember that HMM is a predictive tool, not a guarantee. Hence, always have a strong risk management strategy in place when making investment decisions.

Scenario: Let's imagine that over the past few months, the stock price of Apple Inc. has been oscillating between $150, $175, and $200. The financial analyst has observed a 50% chance of the stock price remaining constant, a 30% chance of it increasing by $25, and a 20% chance of it declining by $25.

Issue: The analyst is aiming to forecast the stock price over the next ten days, with the current stock price standing at $175.

Solution:

Day 1: There's a 50% probability the stock will stay at $175, a 30% probability it will rise to $200, and a 20% probability it will fall to $150. Let's assume the stock stays at $175 (based on the highest probability).

Day 2: Assuming the stock remains at $175, the chances are the same as on Day 1. Let's assume the stock price rises to $200 (based on the second highest probability).

Day 3: With the stock price at $200, there's a 50% chance it will stay at $200, a 30% chance it will drop to $175, and a 20% chance it will drop even further to $150. Let's assume the stock stays at $200 (based on the highest probability).

Day 4: The probabilities are the same as Day 3 since the stock price hasn't shifted. Let's assume the stock falls to $175 (based on the second highest probability).

Day 5 - Day 10: Repeat the above process for the remaining days. Keep in mind this is a basic example. In reality, there are many more factors to consider. The probabilities would be determined from historical data and the Baum-Welch algorithm, not randomly assigned.

This example shows how HMM uses transition probabilities to forecast future states (stock prices). It's important to understand that these forecasts are based on probabilities and may not always accurately predict future stock prices. Therefore, it's vital to use HMM along with other models, and to implement a strong risk management strategy.

Bayesian Network Models

When predicting and measuring stock market prices, probabilistic models are crucial tools. Among the most effective of these in finance is the Bayesian Network Models. These models enable investors and financial analysts to calculate the likelihood of an event happening based on certain circumstances.

Bayesian Network Models, also known as belief networks, are graphical models that illustrate the probabilistic relationships among a group of variables. They are directed acyclic graphs in which nodes represent random variables, and edges represent the conditional dependencies between these variables.

These models are especially useful in finance due to their ability to manage uncertainty and randomness, characteristics inherent in financial markets. Bayesian networks can model the evolving relationships between different variables over time, offering a dynamic and adaptable framework for financial analysts.

For example, a Bayesian network can be used to model the relationship between the economy's overall health, a particular industry's performance, and a specific company's stock price within that industry. This model can then predict the probable future price of the stock given the current economic conditions and industry performance.

Bayesian networks can also handle missing or incomplete data. In the stock market, some information may not be immediately available or may be released at different times. Bayesian networks can integrate this uncertainty into their models, resulting in more robust and realistic predictions.

Another advantage of Bayesian Network Models is their capacity to learn from data. The model can be updated to incorporate new information as more data becomes available. This feature is especially useful in the stock market, where conditions can change quickly and unpredictably.

Bayesian networks are also useful in finance for risk modeling and management. For example, a Bayesian network could be used to calculate the likelihood of a financial crisis based on various economic indicators. By modeling different risk factors' relationships, Bayesian networks can help investors and financial institutions better understand their risk exposure. This understanding can then be used to create strategies to mitigate these risks.

Bayesian Network Models are also excellent tools for stress testing because of their ability to handle uncertainty. Financial institutions use stress testing as a simulation technique to assess their potential vulnerability to certain adverse events. Bayesian networks can model the probability and impact of these events, providing a comprehensive view of potential risks.

However, Bayesian Network Models have their challenges. Building a Bayesian network requires a deep understanding of different variables' relationships, which can be complex and time-consuming, especially when dealing with many variables. Furthermore, while Bayesian networks can manage uncertainty, they may not always capture the complexity and volatility of financial markets. Certain assumptions made by these models may not hold in real-world scenarios, potentially leading to inaccurate predictions.

A Bayesian Network Model is a visual tool that depicts the relationships between a set of variables. It is largely used to comprehend complex systems, allowing us to visualize variable dependencies and make probability-based forecasts. In the stock market scenario, it can be used to predict share prices.

To better understand how Bayesian Network Models can be used in share price prediction, we must consider that share prices are influenced by various factors such as company profits, economic indicators, and geopolitical events, among others. A Bayesian Network Model can consider all these variables and their interconnections, leading to more precise predictions.

Here are the steps an investor can follow to use Bayesian Network Models for stock price prediction:

Identify Pertinent Variables: The initial step requires identifying all potential variables that could affect share prices. These variables could be tangible factors like the company's profits and industry performance, or intangible factors such as market sentiment and geopolitical events.

Build the Bayesian Network: After identifying all pertinent variables, the next step involves creating a Bayesian Network. This includes creating a visual representation of all the variables and their interrelationships.

Calculate the Probability Distributions: The subsequent step involves determining the probability distributions for each variable using historical data.

Train the Model: Once the probability distributions have been determined, the Bayesian Network Model needs to be trained.

This involves inputting historical data into the model, allowing it to 'learn' the interrelationships between variables.

Test the Model: After the training phase, it is crucial to test the model's accuracy. This can be achieved by inputting new data into the model and comparing its predictions to actual results.

Refine the Model: Depending on the test results, the model may need refinement. This could entail adjusting variable relationships or adding new variables.

Use the Model for Prediction: Once the model has been refined and tested, it can be used to predict future share prices.

Regularly Update the Model: As the stock market is dynamic and constantly changing, it is crucial to keep updating the Bayesian Network Model with new data.

Example Situation:

Assume you are an investor looking to forecast the stock price of Company X, a tech sector firm. Your first step would be to pinpoint relevant factors that could influence Company X's stock price. These factors might range from the organization's quarterly earnings, the performance of other tech companies, economic indicators such as unemployment and inflation rates, and global events like trade deals or conflicts.

Following this, you would construct a Bayesian Network Model reflecting these factors and their interconnectedness. For instance, you may discover that the firm's earnings are significantly impacted by the performance of other tech firms and economic indicators.

Next, you utilize historical data to compute the probability distributions for each factor. For example, previous quarterly earnings reports might be used to establish the probability distribution for Company X's earnings.

Once the probability distributions have been determined, this historical data is used to train the Bayesian Network Model. This lets the model 'understand' how the factors interplay and how a change in one factor (like a spike in unemployment) could impact another (like Company X's earnings).

After your model is trained, its accuracy is tested by inputting new data and comparing the model's forecasts to actual outcomes. If the predictions are incorrect, you can fine-tune the model by modifying the factor relationships or introducing new factors.

Once the model has been fine-tuned and tested, it can be used to forecast Company X's future stock prices. However, due to the constant fluctuations in the stock market, it is essential to frequently update the model with new data to ensure its forecasts stay accurate.

Effective Methods:

Consistently Track Pertinent Factors: Monitor all the factors that influence the price of your selected stock. This covers not just company-specific factors, but also wider economic and global events.

Regularly Refresh Your Model: Given the dynamic nature of the stock market, it is essential to regularly update your Bayesian Network Model with new data to maintain the accuracy of your forecasts.

Employ Multiple Models: To enhance forecast accuracy, think about using several Bayesian Network Models, each concentrating on different groups of factors.

Assess and Fine-tune Your Model: Regularly compare your model's forecasts with actual outcomes and fine-tune it as needed. This could require modifying factor relationships or introducing new ones.

Begin Small: Start by investing a small sum based on your model's forecasts. As your faith in the model's accuracy grows, you can slowly increase your investment.

Broaden Your Portfolio: Even the most accurate model cannot forecast the future with absolute certainty. Diversify your investment portfolio to spread risk and boost potential returns.

Let's take a basic instance of applying a Bayesian Network Model to predict stock prices. Suppose we aim to forecast the share price of Tech Company X, and we've identified three main factors that affect its value: the company's quarterly earnings (E), performance of other tech firms (T), and the unemployment rate (U). Historical data shows probabilities of good/bad earnings, good/poor tech performance, and low/high unemployment rates as 0.6/0.4, 0.7/0.3, and 0.7/0.3, respectively.

Using this information, we can build a Bayesian Network Model, assuming that the stock price of Company X is directly influenced by its earnings and other tech companies' performance and indirectly by unemployment rate. Then, we can compute joint probabilities using historical data. For instance, the joint chance of good earnings and good tech performance could be $0.6 \times 0.7 = 0.42$, or 42%.

Let's say we find that when both earnings and tech performance are good, the stock price of Company X increases 90% of the time. Thus, the conditional probability of the stock price rising under these conditions, P(S+ | E+,T+), is 0.9.

To predict future stock prices, we can update these probabilities with fresh data. For example, if good earnings and strong tech performance persists into the next quarter, the model forecasts a 90% chance of an increase in stock price.

However, this is a simplified model, and real-world scenarios would require consideration of many other factors and complex relationships. It's essential to understand that while Bayesian Network Models can help make informed predictions, they can't guarantee results due to the inherent unpredictability of the stock market.

In addition, this model doesn't consider the time series aspect of stock price data. The stock's price at a specific time is greatly influenced by previous prices, which would need to be accounted for in a more sophisticated model.

Monte Carlo Simulation

In the world of finance, particularly in stock market analysis, probabilistic models are crucial tools. The Monte Carlo simulation, a widely known and utilized probabilistic model, is used to predict stock prices. The model uses probability theory to anticipate the likely outcome of uncertain events such as future stock prices.

Monte Carlo simulations are named after the renowned Monte Carlo Casino in Monaco, a place where games of chance illustrate the random processes that these simulations emulate. This mathematical method helps us comprehend the inherent risk and uncertainty in predicting future events. It directly uses randomness and relies on repeated random sampling to attain numerical results.

In the stock market context, a Monte Carlo simulation produces numerous potential paths that the price of a stock may follow in the future. Each path signifies a potential world state, with the probability of each state determined by the model inputs. These inputs could include factors like historical stock prices, market volatility, and other market aspects.

The first step in a Monte Carlo simulation is to outline a stock price model. This could be a straightforward model presuming the stock price follows a geometric Brownian motion, or a more intricate model considering factors like dividends and interest rates.

Once the model is outlined, the simulation generates numerous random paths for the stock price. Each path reflects a possible future for the stock price, and the model determines the probability of each path. This collection of paths constitutes a distribution of potential future stock prices.

The output of a Monte Carlo simulation isn't a single future stock price prediction, but a probability distribution of potential future prices. This distribution can be used to calculate metrics such as the stock price's expected value, the probability that the stock price will exceed a certain level, or the Value at Risk (VaR).

Monte Carlo simulations' primary benefit is their adaptability. They can model complex financial instruments with various types of uncertainty, like future volatility of the stock price, future dividends, or future interest rates.

Another benefit of Monte Carlo simulations is their ability to model non-linear relationships between variables. This is especially significant in finance, where many instruments' payoffs are non-linear functions of their underlying assets.

However, Monte Carlo simulations also have drawbacks. They require numerous simulations to yield accurate results, which can be computationally intensive. Moreover, the results' accuracy heavily relies on the accuracy of the inputs and the used model.

The Monte Carlo Simulation is a computational algorithm that leverages randomness to address problems, regularly employed in estimating results within a specific range. This makes it a handy tool for forecasting stock price volatility. Predicting stock prices is a crucial function in the financial world, and its unpredictable nature has resulted in the creation of several methods, including the Monte Carlo Simulation, to forecast future prices by simulating a range of possible outcomes.

To effectively use the Monte Carlo Simulation, you need to understand the concept well - it uses historical stock prices and probability to predict future prices. The first step entails gathering historical data, which is then used to compute the statistical properties of the stock price, such as mean and standard deviation. Next, a mathematical model that describes the stock price behavior is created, taking into consideration the calculated statistical properties. Simulations are then run, generating random numbers that represent potential future stock prices. The accuracy level you aim to achieve determines the number of simulations run.

After running the simulations, analyze the results by calculating the probabilities of different outcomes and using them to predict future stock prices. This process is iterative - you have to repeat the steps several times to improve prediction accuracy. Once the predictions are ready, you can incorporate them into your investment decisions.

Monte Carlo simulations can revolutionize investing by leveraging computational statistics to predict a range of potential outcomes, giving investors a comprehensive view of stock market volatility and risk. They are mainly used in finance for risk assessment, portfolio optimization, option pricing, strategy determination, continuous improvement, understanding risk tolerance, portfolio diversification, benchmarking, decision making, data updating, back-testing, confidence building, and future planning.

By running thousands or millions of simulations, investors can understand the likelihood of different outcomes, simulate the performance of various investment portfolios, and better assess the value of an option by simulating potential future price movements of an underlying asset.

The results of the Monte Carlo simulations can guide you in diversifying your portfolio, understanding your risk tolerance, and forming your investment strategy. It's crucial to remember that as market conditions vary, simulations should be updated to reflect these changes. Regular data updating ensures that the simulations stay accurate and relevant. You can also use the Monte Carlo simulations to back-test your investment strategies, improve your confidence in your investment decisions, and plan for the future.

Let's suppose you're an investor considering investing in Apple Inc. and you wish to forecast the company's stock price for the upcoming year. You can apply the Monte Carlo Simulation in this real-world situation as follows:

Gather Past Data: Obtain historical prices of Apple Inc. shares from a trustworthy financial data provider. This information is crucial for calculating the average and standard deviation, essential components for constructing your model.

Determine Statistical Characteristics: After obtaining the past data, work out the average and standard deviation of the stock prices. These values will be used as inputs in your Monte Carlo Simulation model.

Construct a Mathematical Model: Use the computed average and standard deviation to create a mathematical model that replicates the behavior of Apple's stock price. This model might be a geometric Brownian motion model, a common model in finance.

Execute Simulations: Perform thousands or even millions of simulations using random numbers. The quantity of simulations you execute depends on the precision level you aim to reach. Each simulation will result in a different possible future price for Apple's stock.

Evaluate Outcomes: Once the simulations are complete, determine the probabilities of various results and use them to predict the future stock price of Apple.

Apply the Forecasts: The predicted range of stock prices can guide your investment choices. If the range is overly volatile or the potential loss is too high, you might need to reconsider investing in Apple.

Ensure to continually update your data and perform new simulations as market conditions fluctuate. This will help maintain the accuracy and relevance of your predictions.

Here are some practical tips on utilizing Monte Carlo Simulation in real time:

Consistently Update Data: Given the ever-changing nature of the financial market, it's vital to regularly update your data to keep your predictions precise and pertinent.

Perform Numerous Simulations: The more simulations you perform, the greater the precision of your predictions.

Experiment with Various Scenarios: Monte Carlo Simulation lets you carry out simulations based on a broad range of scenarios, contributing to a better understanding of the risk and potential return.

Portfolio Diversification: The results can provide guidance on diversifying your portfolio, reducing risk, and maximizing returns.

Test Investment Strategies: The simulations can be used to test your investment strategies, thereby boosting your confidence in your decisions.

Let's use a basic example to demonstrate the Monte Carlo Simulation:

Imagine that Apple's stock (AAPL) currently costs $100. Over the past year, the stock has demonstrated an average return of 8% with a standard deviation of 20%.

To set up the Monte Carlo Simulation, begin with:

Initial stock price (S0): $100

Average return : 8% or 0.08

Standard deviation (σ): 20% or 0.20

Time (t): 1 year

Number of simulations: 1000

Generate random values by using a random number generator to create 1000 random figures. Assume these figures are normally distributed with an average of 0 and a standard deviation of 1.

To calculate the end of the year stock price for each simulation, use this formula:

$$S = S0 \ \exp((r - 0.5\sigma^2)*t + \sigma*sqrt(t)*Z)$$

Where Z is the generated random number.

To determine the expected stock price at the end of the year, calculate the average of all the simulated stock prices.

To analyze the results, determine the likelihood of the stock price being above or below certain amounts. For example, you may wish to know the likelihood of the stock price exceeding $120 or falling below $80.

You can use these probabilities to make knowledgeable investment decisions. For instance, if there's a high likelihood of the stock price exceeding $120 from the simulation, you might consider investing in AAPL. Conversely, if there's a high chance of the stock price falling below $80, you may want to refrain from investing in AAPL or consider selling if you already possess AAPL shares.

Keep in mind, this is a simplified example. In real life, you'd also have to take into account other factors such as dividends, interest rates, and other market conditions. The more simulations you perform, the more precise your predictions will become.

Autoregressive Moving Average (ARMA)

Probabilistic models are essential in finance, particularly for forecasting stock prices. A common model is the Autoregressive Moving Average (ARMA), which incorporates two methodologies - autoregressive (AR) and moving average (MA) - to predict future values based on historical ones.

The AR component of the ARMA model uses past values in the time series to forecast future ones, assuming current stock prices have a correlation with past prices. This aspect is beneficial in stock price forecasting, where past trends often give insights on future movements.

On the other hand, the MA component of the ARMA model employs a moving average, a prevalent tool in technical analysis. This average smooths the price data to identify trends by removing the "noise" from random short-term price fluctuations. In the ARMA model, it compensates for the random variation in the series.

Essentially, the ARMA model is a tool to comprehend and predict future points in the series. In terms of stock prices, this could mean forecasting the next day's price based on the past few days' prices and errors.

It's crucial to remember that the ARMA model depends on stationary data, where the data properties remain unchanged over time. In terms of stock prices, this often implies detrending or differencing the data to eliminate any underlying trends or seasonality.

The ARMA model's flexibility and accuracy have made it popular in econometrics and finance. It enables the modeling of different time series patterns, making it a versatile tool for financial forecasting.

However, the ARMA model does have its shortcomings. As a linear model, it may not capture complex nonlinear relationships that may exist in financial data. Furthermore, the requirement for data to be stationary can be a significant limitation, especially with stock prices that often display trends and non-constant variance. Despite these drawbacks, the ARMA model remains a preferred choice for forecasting stock prices due to its simplicity and interpretability. It's a sturdy and adaptable model that's easy to implement and interpret, making it a practical tool for financial analysts.

Also, ARMA model extensions like the ARIMA (Autoregressive Integrated Moving Average) and GARCH (Generalized Autoregressive Conditional Heteroskedasticity) models have been created to manage non-stationary data and changing variances, further enhancing its applicability in financial forecasting.

The Autoregressive Moving Average (ARMA) is a statistical method utilized for time series analysis. It merges the Autoregressive (AR) model and the Moving Average (MA) model for predicting future data points based on past ones. In the stock market context, ARMA can be an essential tool for forecasting future stock prices using historical data. This guide will explain how to use this model to improve your investment decisions.

To begin with, understanding the two components of the ARMA model is necessary. The Autoregressive (AR) model forecasts future stock prices using the prices from previous times. Conversely, the Moving Average (MA) model uses the error rates from past periods to predict future prices.

Collect historical data of the particular stock prices you're interested in as the first step. Various financial websites or platforms provide this data. Make sure you have enough data to make the model more dependable.

Then, determine the order of both the AR and MA models you plan to apply. The AR model's order refers to the amount of past data the model will use, whereas the MA model's order refers to the count of error rates from past periods the model will consider. Statistical measures like the Akaike Information Criterion (AIC) or the Bayesian Information Criterion (BIC) can guide this decision.

Next, estimate the ARMA model's parameters after deciding the AR and MA models' order. Different estimation methods, like Maximum Likelihood Estimation (MLE) or Least Squares Estimation (LSE), can be used to achieve this. The aim is to find the best fitting parameters for the historical data.

After estimating the parameters, the ARMA model can be used to create future stock price forecasts. Remember that these predictions are probabilistic, meaning they have a degree of uncertainty, but they can offer a useful guide on probable stock price trends.

The ARMA model can also provide interval forecasts in addition to point forecasts. These are the ranges within which future stock prices are expected to fall with a particular probability. Interval forecasts can offer a measure of the uncertainty linked to point forecasts.

It's critical for investors to remember that the ARMA model, like all models, is only as accurate as its foundational assumptions. The model supposes that the process creating the stock prices is stationary, implying that the mean and variance of the process stay constant over time. If this assumption is incorrect, the ARMA model's predictions may be faulty.

Additionally, the ARMA model doesn't consider other information that could affect stock prices, like economic news, company announcements, or market sentiment shifts. Therefore, it's important to use the model alongside other analysis forms. Finally, it's vital to regularly update the ARMA model with new data. This will help you to identify any changes in the underlying process and make more precise predictions.

Let's imagine a scenario where you are an investor interested in the tech sector and want to forecast Apple's future stock prices, based on the information provided.

Firstly, you'll need to gather historical data on Apple's stock prices. This information can be sourced from financial platforms such as Yahoo Finance or Google Finance. It's beneficial to have several years' worth of data to ensure the reliability of your forecasting model.

Secondly, you'll need to establish the order of the AR and MA models. Statistical tools like the Akaike Information Criterion (AIC) or the Bayesian Information Criterion (BIC) are useful for making this decision. A lower score in AIC or BIC suggests a superior model.

Once you've determined the order of the AR and MA models, you'll need to estimate the parameters of the ARMA model. Techniques such as Maximum Likelihood Estimation (MLE) or Least Squares Estimation (LSE) are helpful in this process. The aim here is to find the parameters that best suit the historical data.

With the parameters estimated, you can now use the ARMA model to predict future stock prices of Apple. Bear in mind, these are probabilistic forecasts and come with a degree of uncertainty. Nonetheless, they can provide a helpful insight into potential stock price trends.

Additionally, the ARMA model can provide interval forecasts. These are ranges within which future stock prices are likely to fall, based on a specific probability. This information can help you understand the potential risk associated with your investment.

It's essential to update your ARMA model regularly with new data to spot any changes in the underlying process and enhance the accuracy of your predictions.

Lastly, remember that the ARMA model doesn't factor in aspects like economic news, company announcements, or shifts in market sentiment. Therefore, it's crucial to combine the predictions from the ARMA model with other analyses to make well-informed investment decisions.

We'll illustrate the ARMA model's functioning for stock price prediction using a straightforward example. We'll resort to fabricated data for the sake of ease; however, real-life applications would require genuine historical stock price data.

Consider the last 5 days' data of Apple's stock prices:
Day 1: $150, Day 2: $152, Day 3: $155, Day 4: $153, Day 5: $156.
Our aim is to predict the stock price for Day 6.

Step 1: Determine the AR and MA models' order. For this example, we'll operate under the assumption that we're utilizing an ARMA(1,1) model. This implies we're considering the previous day's stock price (AR order of 1) and the preceding day's error term (MA order of 1).

Step 2: Evaluate the ARMA model's parameters. Let's say we've estimated these parameters to be 0.9 for the AR term and 0.5 for the MA term for argument's sake. These figures would usually be determined through techniques like Maximum Likelihood Estimation (MLE). However, we've just selected random numbers for this example.

Step 3: Use the ARMA model for Day 6's stock price prediction.
The ARMA(1,1) model formula is as follows:
Prediction = Constant + (AR coefficient x previous day's price) + (MA coefficient x previous day's error)

Assuming a constant of zero (for ease) and using our estimated coefficients, we can predict the Day 6 price:
Prediction = 0 + (0.9 x $156) + (0.5 x error)

The error term is calculated based on the difference between your model's prediction and the actual price for the previous day. Let's assume the error for Day 5 was $1 for the sake of simplicity.

So, Prediction = 0 + (0.9 x $156) + (0.5 x $1) = $140.4 + $0.5 = $140.9. Therefore, according to our ARMA(1,1) model, the predicted stock price for Day 6 is approximately $140.9.

Keep in mind, this is an oversimplified example. Real-life stock price prediction would require more intricate models, larger data sets, and additional factors not examined in this model.

Random Walk Models

The random walk model is a frequently used probabilistic model for determining stock prices. It suggests that the future price of a stock doesn't depend on its past prices, with each price change being a random deviation from the last price. The model likens the path of stock prices to a drunk person's walk, with each step taken in a random direction independent of the previous one. This theory aligns with the efficient market hypothesis (EMH), which posits that stock prices at any time fully represent all available information. Consequently, the EMH suggests that no analysis can provide an investor with a market advantage as the market instantaneously integrates all information into the stock prices.

Although the random walk model is simple and comprehensible, suggesting that the best prediction of a stock's future price is its current price with a random error term, it might not always be perfectly accurate. However, it serves as a beneficial benchmark for comparing other complex models.

The model makes several assumptions. First, it assumes that the series of price changes have a constant mean and variance over time, implying that price changes are normally distributed, which might not be the case in real-world stock markets. Second, it assumes price changes are independent which contradicts real-world observations of trends or momentum in stock prices. Despite these drawbacks, the random walk model has proven reasonably accurate in predicting stock prices behavior and is often used as a benchmark in developing and testing more complex models. Examples of such models are the autoregressive model, which considers the possibility of autocorrelation in the data, and the moving average model, which is based on the average of past prices.

There are other types of probabilistic models for determining stock prices that factor in external elements like macroeconomic indicators, company earnings, and investor sentiment. Models like ARCH (Autoregressive Conditional Heteroskedasticity) and GARCH (Generalized Autoregressive Conditional Heteroskedasticity), which allow for variances over time, can be particularly useful in explaining the volatility clustering frequently noticed in stock prices.

The Model: A basic Random Walk Model, in the realm of finance, suggests that stock price changes are random. This infers that future price changes are uncorrelated with past price changes. The future trajectory of a security's price is as unpredictable as a sequence of coin flips.

Data Collection: The first step in applying a Random Walk Model is gathering historical stock price data. This data can be sourced from financial news websites, stock market databases, or financial market research firms.

Data Preparation: After data collection, it needs to be readied for analysis. This includes data cleaning, handling missing values, and arranging the data in a format appropriate for analysis.

Model Implementation: The following step involves implementing the Random Walk Model. This requires a series of calculations to ascertain the random walk. The most prevalent method involves using lagged price changes as the random component.

Model Testing: Post-implementation, it's essential to test the model's accuracy. This generally involves using a subset of your data (the 'holdout set') to gauge the model's performance.

Model Refinement: Depending on the results of the testing, the model may need refinement. This could entail adjusting calculations, redefining the random component, or even accumulating more data.

Use of Software: Numerous software packages, including R, Python, Excel, etc., can assist in implementing and testing a Random Walk Model. These software often include libraries or packages that streamline the process.

Understanding Limitations: It's crucial to grasp that while Random Walk Models can be used for prediction, they have limitations. The model assumes price changes are random and independent, which may not always be true.

Use in Portfolio Management: Random Walk Models can assist in portfolio management. They aid in comprehending the inherent risk in holding specific stocks and can guide asset allocation decisions.

Use in Risk Management: The Random Walk Model provides insight into the randomness of stock price changes, assisting in risk management.

Frequency of Updates: The Random Walk Model requires regular updates as it depends on historical data. The update frequency will vary based on market conditions and the specific stock under analysis.

Consideration of Market Factors: It's crucial to consider other market factors when using a Random Walk Model. These can include economic indicators, news events, or changes in the company's financial status.

Integration with other Models: The Random Walk Model can be combined with other financial models to potentially enhance prediction accuracy.

Long-term Predictions: While the Random Walk Model can be used for short-term predictions, it's generally unsuitable for long-term forecasts due to the inherent unpredictability of stock price changes.

Interpretation of Results: Results from a Random Walk Model should be interpreted cautiously. It is a common misinterpretation to believe that the model can accurately predict future prices.

Continuous Learning: The financial market is dynamic and constantly changing, necessitating continuous learning and adaptation of models. Stay current with the latest research and developments in financial modeling and prediction.

Ethical Considerations: When using models like the Random Walk to predict stock prices and make investment decisions, it's important to consider the ethical implications. This includes considering potential impacts on stakeholders and ensuring transparency in your methodologies.

Practical Context:

Imagine being an investment firm's portfolio manager with the responsibility of overseeing the firm's tech company investments.

Application:

Your first step involves compiling historical data on tech company stocks over the past five years, which you obtain from financial news sites and databases. Once you've gathered the data, you clean it, address any missing values, and format it for analysis.

Next, you use Python, a programming language favored in finance, to apply the Random Walk Model. You calculate the random walk for each portfolio stock using lagged price changes. To verify the model's precision, you create a 'holdout set' from your data, which is not used during the model's implementation but only for testing its performance. If the results are unsatisfactory, you fine-tune the model. This may mean adjusting the calculations, redefining the random component, or gathering more data.

Besides the Random Walk Model, you also take into account other market-related factors like economic indicators, news events, and changes in the company's financial situation. You combine the Random Walk Model with other financial models to possibly improve prediction accuracy.

You then make use of the outcomes from the Random Walk Model to inform your portfolio management choices. You're aware the model gives insight into the randomness of stock price variations and can help evaluate the intrinsic risk in owning specific stocks.

Practical Approaches:

Consistently update the Random Walk Model: It's vital to frequently update the model due to its reliance on historical data. The update frequency would fluctuate based on market conditions and the specific stock being analyzed.

Use for short-term forecasts: The Random Walk Model is more appropriate for short-term predictions. While it can be utilized for long-term forecasts, the inherent volatility of stock price changes makes it less precise for such predictions.

Interpret outcomes carefully: The results from a Random Walk Model should not be seen as an exact prediction of future prices. The model merely offers insight into the randomness of stock price changes.

Never stop learning: The financial market continually evolves, making it crucial to stay informed about the latest research and advancements in financial modeling and prediction.

Ethical considerations: When utilizing the Random Walk Model to make investment decisions, always consider the potential effects on stakeholders and maintain transparency in your methods.

Suppose you're managing a portfolio containing shares from two tech firms, TechA and TechB. You have historical data from these stocks for the previous five years.

Assuming for simplicity that the stocks display the following traits:

TechA has a daily average return of 0.5% and a standard deviation of 1%,

TechB, on the other hand, has a daily average return of 0.4% and a standard deviation of 1.5%,

We'll use the Random Walk Model to forecast the stock prices for both companies after five trading days (a week).

According to the Random Walk Model, future stock prices are unrelated to previous prices and are calculated by adding a random error to the current price. The equation is as follows:

Future price = Current price + (Current price * Return)
Here, Return is a randomly selected number following a normal distribution with the daily average return and standard deviation. Let's assume that TechA and TechB's current stock prices are $100 and $200 respectively.
For TechA, the price after one day could be:
Price = $100 + ($100 × 0.005) = $100.50
For TechB, it could be:
Price = $200 + ($200 × 0.004) = $200.80
You would repeat this method for five days to get a weekly prediction. The prices will not be the same each time you do the calculation due to the random walk.

Remember, these are simply predictions. The Random Walk Model utilizes randomness and the stock's previous behavior to forecast, so actual prices may differ.

It's also important to note that the Random Walk Model assumes that the market is efficient, meaning that all past information is completely reflected in the current prices. This might not always be true in actual markets, so it's always recommended to use other indicators and tools when making investment decisions.

Mean Reversion Models

Mean Reversion Models are widely utilized in the finance sector, especially in the assessment of stock prices in the stock market. The basis of these models is the presumption that over time, stock prices will return to their mean or average. This model type is used to predict and analyze future stock price movements. The operating principle of the Mean Reversion Model is the notion that extreme prices are temporary and prices usually gravitate towards the mean over time. This implies that when a stock price significantly deviates from its mean, it is expected to return to the mean price eventually. This model is often employed by traders and investors to pinpoint securities that may be under or overvalued.

The theoretical foundation of Mean Reversion Models is rooted in the concept of equilibrium in financial markets. The belief is that market forces will eventually drive prices towards their inherent value or mean. Any external factors causing price deviation are viewed as temporary, and in time, the price will self-correct.

These models are particularly beneficial for short-term predictions as they depend on the statistical phenomena of prices, which generally do not show a steady and consistent pattern in the long run. The main strength of the model lies in its capability to indicate the future direction of stock prices based on historical volatility and price trends.

Mean Reversion Models are also utilized in various trading strategies including pairs trading and statistical arbitrage, where the profit potential lies in the price difference between two correlated securities. In these instances, the Mean Reversion Model aids in identifying when the prices are likely to converge or diverge.

In terms of assessing stock prices, Mean Reversion Models offer a measure of the extent to which the current price deviates from the historical mean. This measure is frequently used as an indicator of overbought or oversold market conditions.

However, in spite of their extensive use, Mean Reversion Models have limitations. One major limitation is their assumption that the mean is a fixed value. In actuality, the mean can vary over time due to factors like changes in the company's fundamentals or broader market conditions.

Another limitation of Mean Reversion Models is their assumption that stock prices follow a normal distribution. In reality, stock prices often exhibit skewness and kurtosis, meaning they can have fat tails and sharp peaks, which are not captured by a normal distribution.

Moreover, Mean Reversion Models rely on historical data and do not consider future events or changes in market conditions. Therefore, they may not accurately predict future stock price movements, especially in volatile markets.

Despite these limitations, Mean Reversion Models continue to be an invaluable tool for traders and investors. They offer a framework for understanding stock price dynamics and can assist in making informed investment decisions.

Mean reversion models are a popular concept used in the financial markets, specifically in predicting stock prices. They are premised on the assumption that high and low prices are temporary and that prices tend to move towards the average or mean over time. This guide aims to provide a practical understanding of how to utilize mean reversion models to predict share prices in the stock market.

The first step in using mean reversion models is understanding the concept of mean reversion. This involves the recognition that the price of a stock will move towards its average or mean value over a certain period. The mean value is usually calculated from historical price data.

Secondly, it's important to identify the mean or average price of the stock. This can be done by calculating the historical average price of the stock over a specific period such as six months, one year, or even five years. The longer the timeframe, the more reliable the mean value tends to be.

Once you have the mean value, the next step is to determine when the stock price deviates significantly from this mean. This deviation can be due to various factors such as market news, financial reports, or changes in the economic environment. The key here is to identify a significant deviation from the mean, which represents a potential trading opportunity.

Next, you need to decide on the degree of deviation from the mean that would trigger a trading decision. This could be a percentage deviation from the mean, or a fixed price difference. This is a critical decision as it will determine your entry point in the trade.

Once you've identified a significant deviation from the mean, the idea is to take a position that bets on the price reverting to the mean. If the price is significantly below the mean, you would buy the stock, expecting the price to rise back to the mean. If the price is significantly above the mean, you would sell or short the stock, expecting the price to fall back to the mean.

It's crucial to set a stop loss at this stage. A stop loss is a predetermined price at which you will close your trade if the price moves against you. This is needed to limit your potential loss if the price does not revert to the mean as expected.

The timing of the trade is also critical. Mean reversion strategies work best in stable markets where prices are more likely to revert to the mean. In volatile markets, prices may deviate significantly from the mean and stay there for an extended period.

It's also essential to monitor the trade closely. Mean reversion is not a 'set and forget' strategy. You need to keep a close eye on market conditions and adjust your strategy as necessary.

While using mean reversion models, it is important to remember that they are based on historical data and assume that past patterns will continue in the future. This may not always be the case. Therefore, it's advisable to use mean reversion models in conjunction with other technical and fundamental analysis tools.

Another important point is to diversify your portfolio. Mean reversion models shouldn't be the only strategy you use. Diversification can help reduce risks and improve returns.

When it comes to choosing the stocks to apply the mean reversion strategy, it's recommended to choose liquid stocks. Illiquid stocks may not revert to the mean quickly, which can result in losses.

Furthermore, be aware of any upcoming news or events related to the stock. Such events can cause significant price movements that may not align with the mean reversion strategy.

Also, consider transaction costs when trading. These costs, including brokerage fees and taxes, can eat into your profits especially if you're making frequent trades.

Remember, patience is key in mean reversion strategies. It may take time for a stock price to revert to the mean, and you may have to endure some losses in the interim.

Finally, always ensure that you are using a risk management strategy. This is crucial to protect your capital from major losses.

Let's say you're monitoring a specific stock, XYZ. Its average historical price over the previous year has been $50. You observe that XYZ's current price has significantly diverged from its average and is now trading at $40 due to temporary market news that doesn't affect the company's intrinsic value. Considering the significant deviation from the average price (20%), you perceive this as a good opportunity to purchase the stock, anticipating the price will return to its average of $50. You also establish a stop loss at $35; if the price drops to this level, you'll sell the stock to minimize potential loss.

In a few weeks, the temporary market news diminishes, and XYZ's price begins to trend back to its average. Once it reaches $50, you decide to sell and secure your profit. Throughout this period, you continuously watch the market conditions and XYZ's performance, prepared to modify your strategy if required. For example, if significant news about XYZ breaks, you would factor that into your strategy as it could substantially influence the stock's price.

During this period, you're also actively trading other stocks with various strategies to diversify your portfolio and reduce risk.

When calculating your potential profit, you account for transaction costs. You also exercise patience during this process, acknowledging that it might take time for the stock's price to return to the average.

Let's analyze this situation with specific figures. Suppose you purchase XYZ stock for $40 per share. You establish a stop loss at $35, which means you'll automatically sell if the stock price drops to this level to minimize your losses. This puts you at risk of losing $5 for each share. Your goal is to sell the stock when it returns to its average price of $50. Therefore, your potential earnings are $10 per share ($50 - $40).

Assume you choose to buy 100 shares of XYZ. Here's the math: You would initially invest $4,000 (100 shares at $40 each). Your greatest risk (if the stop loss is activated) would be $500 (100 shares at a risk of $5 each).

Your possible earnings (if the stock price reverts to $50) would be $1,000 (100 shares at a profit of $10 each).

We must also account for transaction fees. If you're charged a fixed $10 per trade, you'll have to pay this fee twice (once for buying and once for selling), totaling $20.

If you manage to sell at $50, your total profit would be $980 ($1,000 gross earnings minus $20 in transaction fees).

This gives you a return on investment of 24.5% ($980 net earnings divided by a $4,000 initial investment).

Here's a step-by-step guide to the process:

Identify possible outcomes: In this scenario, the stock price may either increase to $50 (favorable outcome), or decrease to $35 (unfavorable outcome).

Compute possible profits or losses for each outcome: If the stock price escalates to $50, you could sell your stocks for a total of $5,000, yielding a profit of $980 ($5,000 - $4,020). Conversely, if the stock price plummets to $35, you could sell your stocks for a total of $3,500, incurring a loss of $500 ($3,500 - $4,000).

Ascertain the probability of each outcome: According to historical data and market analysis, there's a 70% likelihood of the stock price going up (favorable outcome) and a 30% likelihood of it going down (unfavorable outcome).

Compute the anticipated return for each outcome: The expected profit from the favorable outcome is 70% $980 = $686. The expected loss from the unfavorable outcome is 30% $500 = $150.

Calculate the overall expected return by deducting the expected loss from the expected profit: $686 - $150 = $536.

Determine the expected ROI: The expected earnings of $536 divided by an initial investment of $4,000 equals a 13.4% expected ROI. This means you can anticipate, on average, a return of 13.4% on your initial investment.

Exponential Smoothing Models

Predicting stock prices in the stock market often involves the use of probabilistic models, with Exponential Smoothing Models (ESM) being one of the most commonly utilized. ESMs use past data to predict future prices, placing a particular emphasis on the most recent data. These models can be simple or complex, with the more sophisticated versions considering trends and seasonal variations.

ESMs operate on the principle that the future is determined by the past, assigning gradually decreasing weight to past observations as they recede into history. The appeal of this model for many financial analysts lies in its simplicity and its capacity to handle a wide range of data patterns.

The primary advantage of ESMs is their focus on recent observations. In a rapidly changing environment such as the stock market, the most recent information is often the most valuable. By assigning decreasing weights to older observations, the model ensures the most recent trends have a greater influence on the forecast.

Another benefit of ESMs is their adaptability. The model can be adjusted to account for different data patterns, including trends and seasonality. For example, if a stock consistently grows over time, the model can be tweaked to give more weight to this trend. ESMs use a smoothing constant to determine the weights for past observations. The choice of this constant depends on the stock price's volatility. For highly volatile stocks, a smaller constant might be used to prioritize recent observations.

Both short-term and long-term stock prices can be forecasted using ESMs. Short-term forecasts may focus more on recent trends and volatility, while long-term forecasts may consider longer-term trends and seasonal patterns.

Variations of ESMs include the Double Exponential Smoothing Model, which takes into account trends, and the Triple Exponential Smoothing Model, or the Holt-Winters method, which considers seasonality.

However, ESMs do have their limitations. They assume the future will mirror the past, which isn't always the case in the unpredictable stock market. Choosing the right smoothing constants can also be challenging. If not chosen correctly, the model might overemphasize recent trends or fail to accurately capture them.

Nevertheless, ESMs remain a valuable tool in financial forecasting. They offer a simple yet flexible way to predict stock prices, making them a popular choice among financial analysts. But like all forecasting methods, they should be used alongside other tools and techniques for the most accurate predictions. Exponential Smoothing Models (ESMs) serve as a popular and effective tool for forecasting trends in time series data such as stock prices due to their simplicity and user-friendly nature. ESMs work by applying decreasing weights to older data, making recent trends more significant and useful in predicting future stock prices.

To begin using ESMs for stock market predictions, historical data of the particular stock of interest is required. Such data can be easily obtained from online trading platforms or financial websites. Accumulating several years of historical data makes the forecast more meaningful.

After collecting the data, it is then fitted into an exponential smoothing model. This process involves choosing a smoothing constant, known as alpha, which decides the weight given to the latest observation. Alpha's value lies between 0 and 1 and the higher the value, the more weight recent observations hold. The selection of alpha can greatly influence your forecasts and is typically chosen through trial and error or statistical optimization techniques.

The subsequent step involves using the model to predict future stock prices. Simple exponential smoothing (SES), the simplest model, is effective when stock prices lack a clear trend or seasonality. The smoothed statistic for each period is calculated by taking a weighted average of the actual stock price and the predicted price from the preceding period.

However, if the stock prices exhibit a clear upward or downward trend, a model like Holt's linear exponential smoothing model that considers this trend would be more suitable. This model includes two smoothing constants - one for the level and one for the trend.

Moreover, if the stock prices demonstrate a seasonal pattern, Holt-Winters' exponential smoothing model is recommended. This model incorporates three smoothing constants: one for the level, one for the trend, and one for the seasonality.

After model selection and smoothing constants determination, forecasts for future periods can be created. Predicting several periods ahead offers insight into the future path of the stock prices.

One of the main advantages of ESMs is their ability to swiftly adapt to changes in the underlying pattern of the data, making them ideal for predicting stock prices. However, they are not infallible and should be used alongside other forecasting methods due to unpredictable factors that can influence the stock market. It is crucial to regularly evaluate and adjust your model as new data becomes available.

It's also important to remember that ESMs aren't designed to handle sudden, drastic trend changes or to predict prices in highly volatile markets. They work best in stable markets with consistent patterns.

Lastly, while ESMs can be useful for stock price prediction, they shouldn't be the only strategy employed. Always take into account other fundamental and technical analysis methods to make well-rounded investment decisions. The use of exponential smoothing models is merely one method in a successful investor's toolkit.

Scenario: Suppose you're an investor eyeing stocks of Apple Inc. and you've acquired five years' worth of historical data on Apple's stock prices from a finance website.

Strategy: Begin by incorporating this data into an exponential smoothing model. As Apple's stock prices generally lack a definite trend or seasonality, initiate with a Simple Exponential Smoothing (SES) model.

Choose a smoothing constant, alpha, starting with a value of 0.5. This gives more weight to the recent observations.

Use the model to predict future stock prices of Apple. The forecast for the next period is computed by taking a weighted average of the actual stock price and the predicted price from the previous period.

Frequently assess and modify your model as fresh stock price data comes in. For example, if Apple begins to display a distinct upward or downward trend, consider switching to Holt's linear exponential smoothing model.

If Apple's stock prices start exhibiting a seasonal pattern, you might want to use Holt-Winters' exponential smoothing model. Exponential smoothing models aren't flawless and shouldn't be the sole tool for investment decisions. Always consider other fundamental and technical analysis methods.

For instance, if Apple announces a new product, you might want to think about how this could influence their stock prices and adjust your model accordingly. Similarly, significant changes in the economy, like a recession, could affect Apple's stock prices and should also be considered.

Suppose you possess Apple's stock prices for the past five years. To keep things simple, assume that the closing prices for the last five days were:

Day 1: $150
Day 2: $152
Day 3: $154
Day 4: $152
Day 5: $153

You would use the Simple Exponential Smoothing (SES) model to predict the price for Day 6 with the equation:

$$F(t+1) = \alpha \ A(t) + (1 - \alpha) \ F(t)$$

In this equation:

$F(t+1)$ represents the predicted price for the next day,

α is the smoothing constant (alpha, set at 0.5 for this example),

$A(t)$ is the real value at time t,

$F(t)$ is the predicted price for that day.

If there was no prediction for Day 1, we could use the actual price that day. So, the forecast for Day 2 would be:

$$F(2) = 0.5 \times 150 + (1 - 0.5) * 150 = \$150$$

For Day 3, we would use the actual price from Day 2 and our prediction for Day 2:

$$F(3) = 0.5 \times 152 + (1 - 0.5) * 150 = \$151$$

We would repeat this process for Days 4, 5, and beyond.

Logistic Regression Models

Probabilistic models play a critical role in financial forecasting by allowing analysts to predict stock price fluctuations with varying levels of precision. We're going to explore the use of Logistic Regression, a probabilistic statistical model, in predicting stock prices.

Logistic Regression is a predictive model used to analyze the relationship between a dependent binary variable and one or more independent variables of different types. It's widely used in fields like machine learning, medicine, and social sciences. In finance, it's crucial for predicting the future trajectory of a company's stock price.

Logistic Regression Models are statistical models that use a logistic function to model a binary dependent variable. In the context of stock markets, the binary dependent variable could be whether a stock's price will go up (1) or down (0) over a certain period. The independent variables could be various market factors that are likely to affect the stock price.

The logistic function used in these models provides an output between zero and one, which can be interpreted as the likelihood of a specific outcome - in this case, the likelihood of a stock's price going up or down. This makes Logistic Regression Models particularly useful for financial analysts who are often more interested in the probability of different outcomes than in the exact future stock price.

A key strength of Logistic Regression Models in predicting stock prices is their ability to handle non-linear relationships between the dependent and independent variables. This is important in financial markets, where stock prices often show non-linear patterns. The logistic function can map these non-linear relationships, providing a more accurate prediction than linear models.

Further, Logistic Regression Models can handle both continuous and categorical variables, which enhances their versatility in handling various types of market data. This allows analysts to include a wide range of market factors in their models, from macroeconomic indicators to company-specific data.

Logistic Regression Models also have the advantage of being resilient to noise. Stock prices are known for their volatility, influenced by countless factors, many of which are random or unpredictable. Logistic Regression Models can manage this noise to a certain extent, providing more dependable predictions than models that are more sensitive to random fluctuations.

The interpretability of Logistic Regression Models is another factor that makes them appealing for financial forecasting. The coefficients of the independent variables in the model indicate the direction and strength of the relationship with the dependent variable, providing valuable insights into the factors influencing stock prices and helping analysts to understand the underlying market dynamics.

However, Logistic Regression Models do have certain limitations in predicting stock prices. A major challenge is the assumption of linearity in the logit for the independent variables, which may not always apply. They may also struggle with complex interactions between variables or with very high-dimensional data.

Lastly, although Logistic Regression Models provide probabilities of different outcomes, they don't provide a complete probabilistic forecast of future stock prices. Therefore, they are often used alongside other types of probabilistic models like Bayesian models or Gaussian processes, to provide a more comprehensive view of potential future scenarios.

Despite its name, logistic regression is a statistical tool mainly used for predicting categorical outcomes, but it can also be applied in predicting stock market trends, specifically whether a particular share's price will rise (1) or fall (0). This guide will explain how to use logistic regression models for predicting stock prices.

Starting off, logistic regression is a statistical model that employs a logistic function to represent a binary dependent variable. In the context of the stock market, this binary dependent variable could be whether the stock price will rise or fall.

The first step in this process involves gathering historical data on stock prices, which can be easily accessed from financial platforms like Yahoo Finance or Google Finance. This data should include the opening price, closing price, highest price of the day, lowest price of the day, and the volume of shares traded.

The following step involves identifying the dependent and independent variables. The dependent variable is the outcome you want to predict or explain, in this case, whether the stock price will rise or fall the next day. The independent variables are the factors that may impact your dependent variable, which could include the previous day's opening price, closing price, highest price, lowest price, and volume of shares traded.

108

Before running a logistic regression, the stock prices need to be converted into binary form. This involves creating a new column in your dataset that indicates whether the stock price has risen (1) or fallen (0) compared to the previous day.

Once the data is prepared, it can be divided into a training set for building the model, and a testing set to evaluate how well the model performs with new data.

After the data has been split, a logistic regression model can be fitted to the training data. In Python, this can be done using the 'LogisticRegression' function from the 'sklearn.linear_model' library.

The model will produce coefficients for each independent variable. These coefficients can be interpreted as the change in the log odds of the dependent variable for a one unit change in the independent variable, assuming all other variables remain constant.

After the model is constructed, it's time to test its performance using the testing set. The 'predict' method of your model can be used to generate predictions for this testing set.

Alongside predictions, probability scores should also be generated. These scores provide the likelihood that the dependent variable is a '1' (i.e., the stock price will increase). This can be achieved using the 'predict_proba' method.

Once the predictions and probability scores are generated, the model's performance can be evaluated using metrics like accuracy, precision, recall, F1 score, and Area Under the Receiver Operating Characteristic Curve (AUC-ROC).

Bear in mind that the model may make some incorrect predictions, such as predicting a rise in stock price when it actually falls, or vice versa. These errors should be considered when making trading decisions based on the model's predictions.

It's important to note that logistic regression assumes a linear relationship between the logit of the response and the predictors, which may not always be the case with real-world data. Therefore, checking the assumptions of logistic regression and considering more advanced techniques if these assumptions are not met is advisable.

Keep in mind that the stock market is influenced by numerous factors, many of which are difficult to quantify and include in a model. While logistic regression can provide valuable insights, it shouldn't be the only basis for trading decisions.

It's also advisable to regularly update your model with new data to ensure its relevance, as the stock market is constantly changing, and a model based on outdated data may not provide accurate predictions.

Finally, remember that investing in the stock market always comes with risk. While predictive models like logistic regression can aid in making informed decisions, they cannot guarantee profits. Always carry out thorough research and consider seeking advice from a financial advisor before making investment decisions.

Situation:

Suppose you're an investor considering purchasing stocks from a company known as 'XYZ Corp.' You aim to forecast whether XYZ Corp.'s stock price will escalate or depreciate the following day.

Plan:

Data Gathering: Assemble historical data of XYZ Corp.'s share prices from a financial source such as Yahoo Finance or Google Finance. The data should encompass opening price, closing price, peak price of the day, minimal price of the day, and the volume of shares traded.

Variable Identification: The dependent variable is the result you aim to forecast, which is whether the stock price will escalate or depreciate the next day. The independent variables include the opening price, closing price, peak price, minimal price, and the volume of shares traded the previous day.

Data Processing: Transform the share prices into binary representation (1 for escalation, 0 for depreciation). Include a new column in your dataset to signify this.

Data Segregation: Split the data into a training set (for model development) and a testing set (for model assessment).

Logistic Regression: Apply a logistic regression model to the training data using Python's 'LogisticRegression' function from the 'sklearn.linear_model' library.

Coefficients: The model will yield coefficients for each independent variable. These coefficients signify the alteration in the log odds of the stock price escalating for a one unit alteration in the independent variable.

Testing: Assess the model's performance utilizing the testing set. Generate predictions using your model's 'predict' method.

Probability Scores: Generate probability scores, which offer the likelihood that the stock price will escalate, using the 'predict_proba' method.

Model Evaluation: Assess the model's performance using metrics such as accuracy, precision, recall, F1 score, and AUC-ROC.
Model Update: Consistently update your model with fresh data to preserve its relevance.

To gain a better grasp on predicting stock prices, let's examine a hypothetical situation using fabricated numbers. Suppose on a certain day, XYZ Corp's stock opened at $50, closed at $55, hit a high of $57, a low of $49, and a total of 1,000,000 shares were traded. Let's assume we have a previously trained logistic regression model, with estimated coefficients for these variables as follows:

Opening price coefficient: -0.02
Closing price coefficient: 0.03
Peak price coefficient: -0.01
Minimal price coefficient: 0.01
Volume of shares traded coefficient: 0.0000001

To determine the log odds of the rise in the stock price, we input these values into our logistic regression model:

$$\text{Log odds} = -0.02*(\$50) + 0.03*(\$55) - 0.01*(\$57) + 0.01*(\$49) + 0.0000001*(1,000,000)$$
$$= -\$1 + \$1.65 - \$0.57 + \$0.49 + \$0.1$$
$$= \$0.17$$

To convert the log odds into a probability, we use the logistic function:

$$\text{Probability} = \exp(\$0.17) / (1 + \exp(\$0.17))$$
$$= 0.54$$

Therefore, the model predicts a 54% chance that the stock price will rise the next day.

Always remember to evaluate the model's performance using the test set and metrics such as accuracy, precision, recall, F1 score, and AUC-ROC. Additionally, regularly update the model with fresh data to ensure its accuracy.

Naive Bayes Classifier

Financial sectors utilize probabilistic models as essential tools for predicting, simulating, and understanding stock market price behavior. The Naive Bayes classifier is a prevalent probabilistic model in this area. This potent model is based on Bayes' theorem, a principle of probability theory and statistics that outlines the relationship of conditional probabilities of statistical quantities. The model assumes that the value of a certain feature is unrelated to the value of any other feature, given the class variable, which is referred to as the "naive" assumption.

The Naive Bayes classifier, in the context of stock prices, is applied to predict the probability of various market outcomes, like the chance of a stock price rising or falling, based on certain factors or features. The classifier calculates the posterior probability of each class from the input features and considers the class with the highest posterior probability as the most probable outcome. This makes the Naive Bayes classifier particularly useful in high-input-dimensionality situations, like with stock market data.

The Naive Bayes classifier, despite its simplicity, has shown to be effective in predicting stock price movements due to its ability to handle large data amounts and make real-time predictions, both crucial in the fast-paced stock market. However, it has limitations like the assumption of independence among features, which is often not the case in the real world. Additionally, it assumes all features are equally significant, which may not always be accurate in the stock market.

Even with these limitations, the Naive Bayes classifier's simplicity, efficiency, and effectiveness make it a favored tool for predicting stock prices. Other probabilistic models that can be used for stock price prediction include Gaussian processes, Hidden Markov models, and Bayesian networks, each with its own advantages and disadvantages, and the choice depends on the specific task requirements.

The Naive Bayes Classifier is a widely used machine learning algorithm, rooted in the Bayes theorem of conditional probability. It carries the label 'Naive' due to its assumption that all features are independent, an assumption that is often unrealistic in real-world situations. However, it has demonstrated its effectiveness in various applications, such as forecasting stock market prices.

Here's a step-by-step guide on how to utilize the Naive Bayes Classifier for stock market prediction.

Firstly, collect historical stock price data, which should encompass various features like opening price, closing price, high, low, volume, etc. Such data can be sourced from numerous financial websites or APIs that provide stock market data.

Any machine learning project deems data preprocessing as a critical phase. The collected data may include missing values, outliers, or superfluous information. Cleaning and preprocessing the data to make it appropriate for the Naive Bayes model is vital.

During Feature Selection, it's essential to understand that not every collected feature is beneficial for prediction. You need to identify the most relevant features that can influence the stock prices, either through statistical methods or domain expertise.

Next, create the Naive Bayes model using the preprocessed data and selected features. Choose the type of Naive Bayes model—Gaussian, Multinomial, or Bernoulli—that best fits your data.

The model then needs to be trained with your historical data, allowing it to learn the correlation between the features and stock prices.

Following training, evaluate the model's effectiveness by using some of your data as a test set to compare the model's predictions against actual prices.

If the model's performance is unsatisfactory, it may require adjustments to its parameters or the selection of a different Naive Bayes model. It might also be necessary to revisit feature selection and data preprocessing.

Once the model's performance meets your expectations, it can be used to predict future stock prices. Simply input the features for the desired prediction day, and the model will provide the estimated stock price.

Since the stock market is continually changing, it's important to monitor the model's performance frequently and retrain it with recent data.

Risk Management is crucial, as no model can predict stock prices with absolute accuracy. The model's predictions should be used as a guide rather than a guarantee.

While the Naive Bayes Classifier is a potent tool, it's not the only machine learning algorithm effective for stock market prediction. Other models like Linear Regression, Decision Trees, or Neural Networks might be more suitable, depending on your data and needs.

The effectiveness of your Naive Bayes model is heavily reliant on your data's quality and the relevance of your features. Therefore, devote ample time to data collection, preprocessing, and feature selection.

Lastly, to maintain the model's relevance and accuracy in the fluctuating stock market, continuously update it with the latest data and fine-tune it based on its performance.

Let's explore a real-world example where we use the Naive Bayes Classifier to forecast the stock prices of a company, for instance, Apple Inc.

Data Collection: The initial step involves gathering historical data of Apple's share prices. This data should encompass elements like the opening price, closing price, peak and lowest price of the day, and the number of shares exchanged. Websites such as Yahoo Finance or APIs like Alpha Vantage can supply this information.

Data Preprocessing: Once the data is gathered, it needs to be processed. This may involve dealing with missing values, discarding outliers, and normalizing the data to make it fit for the Naive Bayes model.

Feature Selection: Not all gathered features will be beneficial for the prediction. Using statistical methods or sector expertise, identify the most relevant features. For instance, the closing price of the previous day may be more significant than the volume of shares exchanged.

Model Creation: Formulate a Naive Bayes model using the processed data and chosen features. For example, if your data follows a normal distribution, a Gaussian Naive Bayes model may be an appropriate choice.

Model Training: Educate your model using the historical data. The model will comprehend the relationship between the features and the stock prices.

Model Evaluation: Assess the performance of the model by testing it with a subset of your data. Contrast the model's predictions with the actual prices and compute metrics like Mean Squared Error to measure its precision.

Model Tuning: If the model's performance is not up to par, modify its parameters or select a different Naive Bayes model. Reconsider feature selection and data preprocessing if needed.

Prediction: Once the model's performance is satisfactory, employ it to forecast future stock prices. Input the features for the desired day, and the model will deliver the predicted stock price of Apple Inc.

Regular Updates: Considering the unpredictable nature of the stock market, it's crucial to regularly update your model with the most recent data and retrain it.

Risk Management: Keep in mind that no model can forecast stock prices with absolute precision. Use the model's predictions as a guide rather than a certainty, and ensure a risk management strategy is in place. Remember, your model's effectiveness greatly depends on the quality of your data and the relevance of your features. Therefore, give sufficient time to data collection, preprocessing, and feature selection. To illustrate this concept more clearly, let's simplify the scenario. We'll consider a scenario where the only factors we have are the previous day's closing price and whether it rained in New York (where the stock market is based). We're also assuming that the closing price can either increase or decrease.

Firstly, we determine the prior probabilities. According to our historical data, the stock price increased 70% of the time and decreased 30% of the time, giving us

$$P(\text{Up}) = 0.7 \text{ and } P(\text{Down}) = 0.3.$$

Next, we work out the likelihoods. Let's say that on days when it rained, the stock price increased 40% of the time and decreased 60% of the time. Also, if the previous day's closing price was high, the stock price increased 80% of the time and decreased 20% of the time. This gives us $P(\text{Rainy} \mid \text{Up}) = 0.4$, $P(\text{Rainy} \mid \text{Down}) = 0.6$, $P(\text{High} \mid \text{Up}) = 0.8$, and $P(\text{High} \mid \text{Down}) = 0.2$.

Let's now predict the stock price on a day when it's raining and the previous day's closing price was high. Using the Naive Bayes theorem, we have:

$$P(\text{Up} \mid \text{Rainy, High}) = P(\text{Rainy} \mid \text{Up})\ P(\text{High} \mid \text{Up})\ P(\text{Up}) = 0.4 \times 0.8 \times 0.7 = 0.224$$

$$P(\text{Down} \mid \text{Rainy, High}) = P(\text{Rainy} \mid \text{Down})\ P(\text{High} \mid \text{Down})\ P(\text{Down}) = 0.6 \times 0.2 \times 0.3 = 0.036$$

Let's adjust these probabilities to sum to 1:

$$P(\text{Up} \mid \text{Rainy, High}) = 0.224\ /\ (0.224 + 0.036) = 0.862$$

$$P(\text{Down} \mid \text{Rainy, High}) = 0.036\ /\ (0.224 + 0.036) = 0.138$$

The model thus predicts an 86.2% probability that the stock price will increase and a 13.8% probability that it will decrease.

Keep in mind, this is a significantly simplified scenario. Prediction of actual stock prices would involve a larger number of factors and more intricate dynamics.

Gaussian Processes

Probabilistic models play a crucial role in contemporary finance, especially in the stock market, by offering a mathematical structure that enables price and trend prediction, which is vital for both traders and investors. Among these models, Gaussian Processes have shown to be particularly effective.

A Gaussian Process is a form of probabilistic model that uses a group of random variables, with any finite number of them having a joint Gaussian distribution. This kind of model is frequently employed in machine learning and statistics because of its adaptability and accuracy. In the context of the stock market, Gaussian Processes can be used to predict stock prices based on past data.

The main reason Gaussian Processes are employed in the stock market is their capacity to deal with uncertainty. Stock prices are inherently unpredictable and affected by various unpredictable factors, including global economic trends and company-specific news. Gaussian Processes accommodate this unpredictability by providing a range of possible outcomes instead of a single prediction.

This adaptability is further increased by the Gaussian Processes' ability to model non-linear relationships. Stock prices are influenced by many factors in non-linear ways, and Gaussian Processes can capture these intricate dynamics. This makes them an irreplaceable tool for predicting stock prices in complex and volatile markets.

Moreover, Gaussian Processes are highly versatile. They can model a variety of scenarios, from simple linear trends to complex non-stationary behaviors. This versatility makes them an ideal choice for modeling stock prices, which can exhibit a wide range of behaviors.

Gaussian Processes also offer a measure of confidence in their predictions. This is shown by a confidence interval, which gives a range within which the true value is likely to be. This is especially useful in the stock market, where understanding the range of potential outcomes can be as crucial as the prediction itself.

However, the application of Gaussian Processes in the stock market does present challenges. One of the primary issues is computational complexity. Gaussian Processes require a lot of computation, which can be troublesome when dealing with large datasets. Nonetheless, this issue is being mitigated by improvements in computational methods.

Another challenge is selecting the kernel function. The kernel function shapes the Gaussian Process and can significantly impact the model's accuracy. Selecting an appropriate kernel function can be a complicated task, necessitating a thorough understanding of both the model and the data.

Despite these hurdles, Gaussian Processes continue to be a potent tool for modeling stock prices. They offer a degree of flexibility and precision that other types of probabilistic models find hard to achieve. Furthermore, their ability to manage uncertainty and provide confidence intervals makes them particularly suited to the unpredictable nature of the stock market.

Gaussian Processes (GPs) are highly effective machine learning tools that can be utilized for predicting stock market share prices. This guide will walk you through the process of using GPs for stock market predictions in a step-by-step manner.

It's crucial to first comprehend what Gaussian Processes entail. Essentially, a GP is a set of random variables, with any finite number having a joint Gaussian distribution. They are applied in supervised learning circumstances, particularly in regression and probabilistic classification.

The initial step in utilizing GPs for share price predictions involves data collection and preparation. You'll require historical share price data, encompassing opening price, closing price, highest price, lowest price, and volume of shares traded. The more data you have, the more precise your predictions will be. Following this, you need to preprocess the data by eliminating null or missing values and normalizing the data to ensure all variables are on the same scale. This is vital for enhancing your model's accuracy and eliminating bias.

Subsequently, partition your data into a training set and a test set. The training set, typically making up 70-80% of the data, is used to train the model, while the test set evaluates the model's performance.

With your data ready, you can begin constructing your GP model. Python libraries such as Scikit-learn or GPy can be used for this. Start by defining a kernel, a function that outlines the similarity between data points. Numerous kernel types can be used, like linear, polynomial, and Radial Basis Function (RBF), dependent on your data's nature.

After the kernel definition, you can train your GP model using the training data. The model learns by fitting the kernel's parameters to the data, typically via a process known as training or learning, where the log-marginal likelihood is maximized.

Once trained, the model can be used to predict share prices by providing it with the data features you want to predict share prices for. The result is a Gaussian distribution, providing the mean and variance of the predicted share prices.

Bear in mind that GPs offer a distribution over potential values, not just one prediction. This allows you to quantify your prediction's uncertainty, a useful feature in stock market predictions.

After making predictions, evaluate your model's performance by comparing predicted share prices to actual ones in your test set. Common evaluation metrics include the Mean Absolute Error (MAE), Root Mean Squared Error (RMSE), and R-squared.

If your model's performance is unsatisfactory, fine-tuning it by modifying the kernel or optimizing its parameters can be undertaken. This requires a solid grasp of the data and the model.

Challenges in using GPs for stock market predictions include data noise. Influences such as economic indicators, company news, and global events can cause sudden, unpredictable share price fluctuations, which can be seen as noise. One solution is to use a noise kernel in your GP model.

Another challenge is GPs' computational complexity. Training a GP model involves matrix inversion, with a computational complexity of $O(n^3)$, where n is the number of data points. This makes GPs computationally demanding for large datasets. A solution here is to use sparse GPs, which offer a full GP approximation and reduce computational complexity.

Remember, no model can perfectly predict the stock market. GPs are tools designed to assist in making more informed decisions.

Here's an example demonstrating the application of Gaussian Processes (GPs) in forecasting stock prices:

Suppose you're a data analyst in a finance company tasked with forecasting Microsoft's stock prices for the upcoming month. Here's how GPs come into play:

Data Gathering and Preparation: Begin by procuring Microsoft's historical stock prices from the past five years from a trustworthy financial data source. Your dataset should include opening, closing, highest, and lowest prices as well as the daily volume of shares traded.

Data Preprocessing: Proceed by cleaning up the data, eliminating any null or missing values, and normalizing the data to ensure all variables are on a comparable scale.

Data Division: Once the data is cleaned, divide it into a training set (80%) and a test set (20%).

Model Building: Use a Python library such as Scikit-learn to build your GP model. Due to the nature of your data, you choose to employ a Radial Basis Function (RBF) as your kernel.

Model Training: Train your GP model using the training data. The model learns by adjusting the kernel's parameters to the data.

Predictions: With the model trained, it's time to predict the closing prices for the next month. You'll receive a Gaussian distribution as output, providing the mean and variance of the forecasted prices.

Model Evaluation: After predicting, compare these forecasted prices to the actual prices in your test set, using Mean Absolute Error (MAE), Root Mean Square Error (RMSE), and R-squared as your evaluation metrics.

Model Refinement: If the model's performance is below par, refine it by modifying the kernel or optimizing its parameters.

Let's think about a simpler situation where we've logged the closing stock prices of Microsoft for the past five years. Let's assume these prices have been standardized on a scale of 0 to 1.

Using this data, we can use Scikit-learn to train a Gaussian Process (GP) model with an RBF kernel, which is suitable for modeling the smooth fluctuations commonly observed in stock prices. The GP model will learn to adjust the kernel's parameters (length scale and variance) to best fit the data. After training, the GP model will provide a normal distribution of the potential stock prices for each day in the following month, with the mean of this distribution representing the predicted stock price. For example, if the GP model predicts a normal distribution with a mean of 0.6 and a standard deviation of 0.1 for the next day's closing price, this indicates the model predicts the standardized closing price to be around 0.6, with a fluctuation of 0.1. We can evaluate the model's effectiveness by comparing the predicted prices with the actual ones using metrics such as Mean Absolute Error (MAE), Root Mean Square Error (RMSE), and R-squared.

If the model doesn't perform as expected, we can tweak it by changing the kernel or re-optimizing its parameters. This iterative process is continued until the model's performance reaches the desired standard.

Let's imagine a scenario to show how a prediction might be made. Let's say we have gathered and processed historical data for Microsoft's closing stock prices over the last 5 years, and we've standardized these prices on a 0 to 1 scale.

We then use Scikit-learn to train a Gaussian Process (GP) model using an RBF kernel.

Step 1: Model Training

Imagine we've trained our GP model and it has learned the optimum parameters of the kernel (length scale and variance) to fit the data well.

Step 2: Price Prediction

Once trained, the model is utilized to forecast prices for the forthcoming month. To simplify, let's predict the price for the next day. If the model predicts a normal distribution with a mean of 0.6 and a standard deviation of 0.1 for the closing price of the next day, it means the model predicts the standardized closing price to be approximately 0.6, with a variation of 0.1.

Step 3: Model Evaluation

If the actual closing price for the following day is 0.58, we can compute the Mean Absolute Error (MAE) like this:

$$\text{MAE} = |\text{Predicted value - Actual value}|$$
$$= |0.6 - 0.58|$$
$$= 0.02$$

We can also calculate the RMSE. In this instance, as we're only considering one prediction, RMSE will be the same as MAE. Finally, we'll determine R-squared. For this, we require the mean of the actual values. Let's say it's 0.55 for the test period. R-squared is calculated by subtracting the ratio of the Sum of Squared Residuals to the Total Sum of Squares from 1.

$$= 1 - ((0.6-0.58)^2 / (0.58-0.55)^2)$$
$$= 1 - (0.0004/0.0009)$$
$$= 1 - 0.44$$
$$= 0.56$$

Step 4: Model Refinement

Based on these measurements, we can decide whether to refine the model. If the MAE, RMSE are overly high or R-squared is exceptionally low, we might consider adjusting the kernel parameters or re-optimizing other model parameters.

This is a simplified example. In real-world scenarios, we would make multiple predictions, and the evaluation measures would be calculated across all these predictions.

Markov Chain Monte Carlo (MCMC) Methods

In recent times, the world of finance, particularly in the realm of stock market forecasting, has seen a major shift towards probabilistic modeling. This change was brought about by the advent of advanced statistical techniques and computational algorithms. One such technique gaining significant popularity among financial experts is the Markov Chain Monte Carlo (MCMC) method.

The MCMC method is an influential tool for estimating intricate models in finance. It enables professionals to assess the likelihood of future occurrences based on past data, which is a crucial element in forecasting stock market prices. The method is built on the Markov Chain theory, suggesting that future conditions depend only on the current state, not on the previous series of events.

The MCMC method is notably beneficial in stock market prediction as it facilitates the modeling of intricate dynamic processes that drive stock price fluctuations. The random nature of stock prices necessitates a sturdy method that can encapsulate this dynamism. MCMC serves this purpose by allowing the modeling of stock price fluctuations as a random process.

A key benefit of using MCMC methods in stock market forecasting is their capacity to handle high-dimensional data. In the stock market scenario, this refers to a myriad of factors that can affect stock prices, such as company performance, economic indicators, and market sentiment. MCMC methods can effectively navigate this high-dimensional space to offer precise predictions of future stock prices.

Another significant benefit of MCMC methods is their capability to manage uncertainty. Stock market prediction is inherently uncertain due to the unpredictable nature of stock price fluctuations. MCMC methods offer a structure for quantifying this uncertainty, providing finance professionals with a measure of the reliability of their forecasts.

The MCMC method also permits the integration of prior knowledge into the prediction process. This is accomplished through Bayesian statistics, which mixes previous knowledge with current data to make informed predictions about future occurrences. This feature is particularly useful in stock market forecasting, where past stock price data can offer valuable insights into future price fluctuations.

The versatility of MCMC methods is another primary benefit. They can be utilized to estimate a broad range of models, from simple linear regression models to intricate hierarchical models. This versatility makes them a valuable tool for finance professionals, who can customize their models to the specific features of the stock market data they are dealing with.

Despite their numerous advantages, the application of MCMC methods in stock market prediction is not without its challenges. One of the main challenges is the computational demand of these methods, which can be substantial for large datasets. However, advances in computational power and algorithms have made it increasingly viable to employ MCMC methods to large-scale financial data.

Another challenge is the necessity for careful model specification. The success of MCMC methods in predicting stock prices relies on the suitability of the model used. If the model doesn't accurately depict the underlying dynamics of stock prices, the predictions made using this model may not be dependable.

To demonstrate how MCMC can be utilized in forecasting stock prices, it's necessary to initially view the stock market as a multifaceted system with numerous variables. The share price at any given moment is determined by a multitude of factors such as past prices, market sentiment, economic indicators, and company-specific elements. The intricate nature of this system makes MCMC a fitting strategy.

The initial stage in applying MCMC to forecast stock prices involves defining the issue in terms of probability, which includes identifying the variables that influence stock prices and understanding their interplay. This could be achieved through a comprehensive literature review and consultation with industry experts. Once the variables and their interplay are identified, they can be depicted in a probabilistic model like a Bayesian network. Subsequently, we need to establish our preliminary beliefs about these variables. These beliefs represent our initial assumptions about the variable values before we gather any data. For instance, we might assume that the stock price is equally likely to rise or fall. These assumptions should align with our understanding of the variables and their interplay.

After defining the preliminary beliefs, we can start collecting data, such as historical share prices, economic indicators, and other relevant information. This data is then used to update our initial beliefs through a process called Bayesian updating.

MCMC is applied during the Bayesian updating process. Essentially, MCMC is a method used to generate samples from the posterior distribution, which is the updated belief about the variables after considering the data. The samples created by MCMC are utilized to estimate the posterior distribution's properties.

MCMC's advantage is that it enables us to estimate complex distribution properties without solving intricate mathematical equations. We generate several samples and use them to estimate the distribution's properties.

In terms of share price prediction, the posterior distribution properties we might be interested in could be the anticipated future share price, the probability of the share price rising or falling, or the share price's volatility.

After estimating these properties, we can use them to predict future share prices. For instance, if we estimate that the expected future share price is higher than the current price, it might suggest that it's a favorable time to purchase the share.

However, it's crucial to remember that MCMC is a tool, not a guaranteed solution for accurate predictions. Its effectiveness depends on the data quality and the correct application of the probabilistic model. Thus, it's vital to regularly revise and update the model with new data.

It's also important to recognize MCMC's limitations. The method assumes a Markovian probability distribution, meaning the future state relies solely on the present state, not past states. While this assumption may be valid for some variables, it might not be for others, so validating this assumption before applying MCMC is essential.

Lastly, while MCMC is a potent tool for predicting share prices, it shouldn't be the only method used. It's always advisable to employ a mix of methods and cross-validate your predictions using other techniques.

Let's think about a real-world situation where we are predicting stock prices for a company called ABC Corp.

Step 1: Define the problem in terms of probability: After thoroughly reviewing literature and consulting financial experts, determine the factors that affect the stock prices of ABC Corp. These elements might be past prices, market sentiment, economic indicators, and company-specific elements like earnings reports, product launches, and so on.

Step 2: Create initial beliefs: Before collecting any data, make preliminary assumptions about these factors. For instance, you might assume that the ABC Corp's stock price has an equal chance of increasing or decreasing.

Step 3: Gather data: Collect historical stock prices for ABC Corp, along with other pertinent economic indicators and company-specific information.

Step 4: Use MCMC in Bayesian updating: Utilize the collected data to revise your initial beliefs through Bayesian updating. Use MCMC to generate samples from the posterior distribution (the revised belief about the factors after considering the data).

Step 5: Estimate the characteristics of the posterior distribution: For example, you might want to estimate the likelihood of the stock price increasing or decreasing, or the volatility of the stock price.

Step 6: Predict future stock prices: Use the estimated characteristics to predict future stock prices for ABC Corp. For instance, if the predicted future stock price is higher than the current price, it could indicate that now is a good time to buy the stock.

In real-world situations, this process would be a continuous loop. As new data becomes available, it should be used to update the model. It's also essential to validate your predictions using other methods and regularly test the accuracy of your assumptions.

Furthermore, when using MCMC, always be aware of its restrictions. For example, make sure that the Markovian probability distribution assumption (future state depends only on the current state) is applicable to your factors.

Let's assume a hypothetical case where the stock price of ABC Corp relies on two independent factors: the company's earnings and overall market sentiment.

Let's imagine the following situation:

Suppose ABC Corp is due to release its earnings report tomorrow and recent market sentiment has been positive. Our aim is to predict whether ABC Corp's stock price will rise or fall following the report.

We'll start by applying Bayesian updating to revise our initial assumptions in light of new data. Our starting assumption is that there's an equal chance of the stock price going up or down (0.5 probability for both).

We then collect data on ABC Corp's past stock prices, its earnings, and market sentiment for the previous 100 days. After analyzing this data, we revise our assumptions as follows:

A) With good earnings and positive market sentiment, the probability of the stock price going up is 0.7.

B) With poor earnings and negative market sentiment, the probability of the stock price dropping is 0.8.

Let's now apply these probabilities.

Scenario 1: The earnings report is good and market sentiment is upbeat.

Probability of stock price going up = 0.7

Probability of stock price going down = 1 - 0.7 = 0.3

Given that the probability of the stock price going up (0.7) is higher than it going down (0.3), we can infer that the stock price is likely to increase, suggesting it might be a good time to invest.

Scenario 2: The earnings report is poor and market sentiment is down.

Probability of stock price going up = 1 - 0.8 = 0.2

Probability of stock price going down = 0.8

Here, the probability of the stock price going down (0.8) is higher than it going up (0.2), indicating that the stock price is likely to decrease, and investing might not be advisable.

In reality, predicting stock prices involves considering numerous other factors, and the data gathering and analysis process is much more intricate. However, the fundamental concept of using Bayesian updating to revise our assumptions and make predictions remains constant.

Kalman Filter Models

Probabilistic models play a crucial role in the financial sector, especially in predicting stock market trends. One such notable model is the Kalman filter model. These models are primarily used to estimate a system's current state based on past observations, making them incredibly efficient in forecasting stock prices.

The Kalman filter model is a recursive algorithm that uses a series of measurements observed over time. It generates estimates of unknown variables by minimizing the mean squared error, making it an effective tool for predicting future prices of stocks and other financial assets by analyzing previous trends and patterns.

In financial settings, Kalman filters are frequently employed in pairs trading strategies, which match a long position with a short one in two stocks. The filter calculates the divergence between the two stock prices, generating a signal when the divergence significantly deviates from zero, suggesting a trading opportunity.

A key strength of the Kalman filter model is its ability to account for uncertainties and errors that may occur in the measurement or process. This makes it a sturdy tool for predicting stock prices as it can handle the volatility and randomness inherent in stock market data.

The Kalman filter adjusts its estimates as new data arrive. This dynamic updating feature makes it a potent tool for tracking real-time changes in market conditions and stock prices. This flexibility is particularly useful in a volatile market like the stock market, where prices change rapidly.

Important to mention, the Kalman filter model is not limited to predicting a single stock's price but can also analyze and forecast the behavior of entire portfolios. This feature provides a comprehensive perspective on a set of stocks' potential performance, offering valuable insights for informed decision-making.

The ability of the model to handle multi-dimensional data is another reason for its popularity in the financial sector. With the Kalman filter model, various variables that may affect stock prices, such as company earnings, interest rates, and economic indicators, can be monitored simultaneously.

However, it's crucial to remember that the Kalman filter model's performance, like any other model, is dependent on the accuracy of its initial parameters. Therefore, ensuring the initial parameters

126

are as precise as possible is vital to achieve the most reliable predictions.

The complexity of the Kalman filter model can also be a disadvantage, especially for those unfamiliar with advanced statistical models. It involves various mathematical equations and computations, which may seem overwhelming to beginners.

The Kalman filter is a potent statistical instrument with various applications, including forecasting stock market prices. This method, based on stochastic processes and estimation theory, provides a systematic approach to predicting future values of interest. This guide will help you understand how to use the Kalman filter for stock price prediction.

First, it's important to understand what the Kalman filter is. Named after Rudolf E. Kálmán, the Kalman filter is a recursive algorithm designed to estimate a system's evolving state using incoming, imperfect measurements. In the context of the stock market, the "system" refers to the market itself, and the "measurements" refer to the share prices.

The initial step in employing the Kalman filter for predicting stock prices is to gather historical data of the relevant stocks. This data is used to train the Kalman filter, enabling it to understand the underlying patterns of the share prices. You can usually obtain this data from financial websites or directly from the stock exchange.

Next, you have to create a system model. For stock price prediction, this model could range from a simple linear trend model to a complex dynamic stochastic general equilibrium model. The model chosen depends on the specific traits of the stock being analyzed and the assumptions you're prepared to make.

After the system model is defined, the next task is initializing the Kalman filter. This involves setting initial values for the state and covariance estimates. These initial values can significantly affect the Kalman filter's performance, so it's crucial to select them wisely.

The actual prediction process with the Kalman filter comprises two steps: the prediction and update steps. In the prediction step, the Kalman filter uses the system model to forecast the system's next state and the uncertainty of that prediction. In the context of the stock market, this would be the predicted next share price and its uncertainty.

The update step follows the prediction. Here, the Kalman filter uses the actual observed share price to update its state and covariance estimates. This allows the Kalman filter to learn from its errors and adjust its predictions accordingly.

A key advantage of the Kalman filter is its capacity to deal with noisy data. Stock prices are notoriously volatile, influenced by numerous factors, resulting in considerable noise in the data. The Kalman filter effectively separates the signal from the noise, yielding more accurate predictions.

Another benefit of the Kalman filter is its recursive characteristic. This means it only requires the last state estimate and the current data point to generate the next state estimate, making it highly efficient for real-time applications like intra-day stock price prediction.

However, it's important to note that the Kalman filter, while powerful, is not foolproof. The stock market is influenced by numerous variables, many of which cannot be accurately modeled or predicted. Therefore, Kalman filter predictions should always be used in combination with other analysis methods and tools.

The performance of the Kalman filter heavily depends on the accuracy of the system model. If the model doesn't accurately capture the stock prices' dynamics, the Kalman filter's predictions may be inaccurate. Therefore, it's crucial to invest time in developing and refining the system model.

Additionally, while the Kalman filter can manage data noise, it assumes that the noise is Gaussian. If this assumption is inaccurate, the Kalman filter's performance may be compromised. Thus, it may be necessary to preprocess the data to ensure it fits this assumption.

One way to evaluate the performance of the Kalman filter is by using a hold-out validation set. This is a dataset not used in training the Kalman filter and is used to assess the filter's ability to predict unseen data.

Let's look at a real-world example. Imagine we want to forecast the stock prices of a company called "XYZ" on the New York Stock Exchange (NYSE). Here's how we would go about it:

Data Gathering: Our initial step would be to gather historical data for XYZ's share prices. We could gather this information from financial websites such as Yahoo Finance, Google Finance, or directly from the NYSE.

Building the System Model: We would then construct a system model that closely aligns with the behavior of XYZ's shares. For example, if XYZ's shares have a stable upward or downward trend, a basic linear trend model might suffice. However, if the share prices are affected by multiple factors and are more complex, we may need a more advanced model.

Setting up the Kalman Filter: After the system model is built, we would set up the Kalman filter. This includes setting initial values for the state (the starting share price) and the covariance estimates (the beginning uncertainty).

Prediction and Update Phases: Once set up, we can begin the prediction process. We use the Kalman filter to estimate the next share price of XYZ and the uncertainty of that prediction. When the actual share price for the following day is known, we use this data to revise our state and covariance estimates. This allows the Kalman filter to learn from its mistakes and refine its predictions.

Evaluating Performance: Ultimately, we would assess how well our Kalman filter performed. This can be done using a hold-out validation set - a collection of share prices not used in training the filter. We'd compare the filter's forecasts to this data to assess its ability to predict unseen data.

Practical strategies for real-time prediction include:

Ongoing Updates: The recursive nature of the Kalman filter makes it perfect for real-time prediction. Hence, new share price data should be used immediately to revise the filter's state and covariance estimates.

Layered Approach: While the Kalman filter is potent, it shouldn't be your only tool. It's advised to use it alongside other analytic methods and tools.

Model Refinement: If the Kalman filter's predictions are regularly off the mark, it could indicate that the system model isn't accurately representing the dynamics of XYZ's share prices. In such cases, the model should be refined or a different model should be used.

Data Preprocessing: If the noise in the share price data isn't Gaussian, it could adversely affect the performance of the Kalman filter. In such cases, data preprocessing techniques could be used to make the noise more Gaussian-like.

To illustrate how the Kalman Filter could be used in forecasting stock prices, consider a basic hypothetical scenario based on probability: Suppose stock XYZ is currently priced at $100 and we initially estimate a daily increase of $1. We configure the Kalman Filter using an initial state of $100 (the present stock price) and an initial covariance (uncertainty) value of 10, which signifies our initial prediction uncertainty.

Now, assume the real stock price on the following day is $102. The Kalman Filter will revise its forecast based on this new information. If, for instance, the prediction error covariance (the Kalman gain, or 'K') is 0.5, the updated prediction would be calculated as follows:

New prediction = Previous prediction + K * (actual price - predicted price)

= $101 + 0.5 * ($102 - $101)

= $101.5

Hence, the Kalman Filter would forecast the next day's stock price to be $101.5, not $102.

As it continues to collect data over time, the Kalman Filter will constantly refine its forecasts based on the actual stock prices observed, thereby improving the accuracy of its predictions.

Long Short-Term Memory (LSTM) Models

Probabilistic models are a novel and growing method for forecasting market trends. The Long Short-Term Memory (LSTM) model, a type of recurrent neural network (RNN), stands out for its efficacy. It has an edge over other models due to its capacity to recall past data, making it beneficial for time-series data like stock prices. Unlike conventional linear models, LSTM can identify intricate, non-linear correlations between variables.

This is especially useful in finance, where stock prices are determined by numerous factors. The ability of the model to comprehend these intricate correlations makes it a potent tool for predicting future stock prices.

The LSTM model functions by employing memory cells, enabling it to store and recall data over extended periods. This is vital in the stock market, where past trends frequently impact future price movements. The LSTM model can make more precise predictions about future stock prices by recalling past trends.

LSTM models also have the advantage of avoiding the issue of vanishing or exploding gradients, which is common in conventional RNNs. This enables LSTM models to learn from data over a longer period, making them more precise over extensive time series data like stock prices. LSTM models are also capable of effectively managing noisy data, which is common in stock prices due to unpredictable events.

In addition to predicting stock prices, LSTM models can also be utilized for risk management. By forecasting possible price movements, they can assist traders and investors in managing their risk exposure and making more informed decisions about when to buy or sell stocks.

LSTM models can also be trained on various types of data, not just historical price data. They can analyze news articles, social media posts, and other types of text data to detect sentiment that could impact stock prices, making them even more adaptable for predicting stock market trends.

However, there are some limitations to LSTM models. They can be computationally intensive and require a significant amount of data for effective training. This can make them less appropriate for small-scale trading operations or situations where quick decisions are necessary. Overfitting is another risk with LSTM models. This occurs when the model becomes too complex and begins to fit the noise in the data rather than the trend.

Regularization techniques can be used to counter overfitting, but careful tuning is required.

Despite these challenges, LSTM models have shown promising results in predicting stock prices. Numerous studies have highlighted their ability to outperform other models, making them a valuable tool for traders and investors.

LSTM (Long Short-Term Memory) models are a type of recurrent neural network with feedback connections, making them highly effective for predicting sequences. They are particularly useful in predicting stock prices, which is essentially time series data. This guide will assist you in understanding and implementing LSTM models for stock price prediction.

It's crucial to comprehend how LSTM operates. Unlike conventional neural networks that struggle to recall inputs from far back, LSTM networks have a 'memory cell' that can retain information for extended periods, making them ideal for time-series prediction.

First, gather your data. Past stock prices serve as the model's training data. The more data you have, the more accurately the model can forecast future prices.

After gathering your data, pre-process it to remove any unnecessary information or 'noise', normalize it, and convert it into a format suitable for the LSTM model. This often involves creating a sliding window of input and output data.

You can now commence building your LSTM model. The Keras library in Python simplifies this process. The initial layer in your network should be an LSTM layer with adjustable parameters such as the number of neurons and the activation function.

Next, compile your model by selecting a loss function and an optimizer. The loss function assesses the model's performance, while the optimizer strives to reduce this loss.

Once the compilation is done, adapt the model to your training data. This includes specifying the number of epochs and the batch size. After training, evaluate the model's performance by testing it on new data.

To enhance your model's performance, adjust parameters like the number of neurons in the LSTM layer, the activation function, and the number of epochs. Adding additional layers, such as dropout layers, can help prevent overfitting.

Once the model performs satisfactorily, use it to predict future stock prices. But bear in mind that stock price prediction is inherently uncertain, and even the best model can't guarantee future results. Therefore, LSTM models should be used as part of a larger toolkit.

Remember, LSTM models are only as reliable as the data they're trained on. If the stock market changes in unexpected ways, the model's predictions may not be accurate. Stay informed about the latest research in machine learning as techniques and best practices constantly evolve.

While predicting stock prices with LSTM models can be complex, it can also yield great rewards by helping you make informed decisions. However, LSTMs can't account for sudden changes due to unforeseen factors, so it's crucial to use them in combination with other types of analysis.

Lastly, while this guide focuses on stock prices, LSTM models can be applied to any time-series data, from weather forecasts to sales predictions, making them a highly adaptable tool in machine learning.

Imagine this: You're an investor who's been in the stock market for some time and are looking to apply machine learning to forecast future stock prices and enhance your investment approach.

To begin with, you collect historical stock price data from a trusted source such as Yahoo Finance or Google Finance. You concentrate on a few specific stocks and gather data from the last five years.

Once the data collection is complete, you preprocess it. This could involve eliminating redundant data, dealing with missing values, and normalizing the data to a standard scale. You also form a time-series sliding window of input and output data, which will be utilized in the LSTM model.

Following that, you employ Python and the Keras library to construct your LSTM model. You commence with a single LSTM layer having a certain number of neurons, and try out different activation functions. You compile the model with a loss function of mean squared error using the Adam optimizer.

Next, you fit the model to your preprocessed training data. You decide to train the model for 50 epochs with a batch size of 32, while monitoring the model's performance on a validation set.

After training, you assess the model's performance on a distinct test set, which hasn't been seen by the model during training. You examine metrics like mean squared error and mean absolute error to determine the model's accuracy in predicting stock prices.

You proceed to fine-tune your model, experimenting with varying numbers of neurons, activation functions, and adding dropout layers to prevent overfitting. You also adjust parameters like batch size and number of epochs. Finally, once you're content with your model's performance, you use it to forecast future stock prices for the stocks you're interested in. You incorporate these predictions into your overall investment strategy, but you also rely on other types of analysis and stay informed about pertinent news that could influence stock prices. Absolutely, let's devise a straightforward example to comprehend the application of the LSTM model in predicting stock prices. Consider we have the closing stock prices for a specific company for seven consecutive days as follows:

Day 1: $100
Day 2: $102
Day 3: $105
Day 4: $107
Day 5: $110
Day 6: $112
Day 7: $115

We'll utilize this data to educate our LSTM model. For this particular instance, we'll employ a basic LSTM model with a single hidden layer and one output layer. To establish a suitable sequence for the LSTM model, we'll implement a sliding window of three days. This implies that we'll employ the stock prices of three successive days to anticipate the price for the fourth day.

Our input and output sequences will appear as follows:

Input: [100, 102, 105], Output: [107]
Input: [102, 105, 107], Output: [110]
Input: [105, 107, 110], Output: [112]
Input: [107, 110, 112], Output: [115]

We'll then input these sequences into our LSTM model for training. Once trained, the model will be capable of discerning the pattern in the stock price fluctuations and utilize this to make future predictions. Let's assume we want to predict the stock price for day 8. We'll employ the stock prices from days 5, 6, and 7 as input: Input: [110, 112, 115]. After processing this input, our LSTM model may predict that the stock price for day 8 will be $118. This is an overly simplified instance, and real-world stock price prediction would involve considerably more complicated models and larger datasets.

Autoregressive Conditional Heteroskedasticity (ARCH)

The area of financial market analysis is consistently advancing with the development of complex probabilistic models. The Autoregressive Conditional Heteroskedasticity (ARCH) model has become increasingly popular in recent years as a crucial tool in gauging stock prices in the stock market, especially in identifying the instability and unpredictability inherent in financial assets. The ARCH model, first brought forth by Robert Engle in 1982, is a time-series model primarily used to predict financial market volatility. It's designed to identify 'volatility clustering' - a common characteristic seen in stock market returns where periods of high volatility follow each other and vice versa.

The ARCH model's main premise is that the current error term or residual's variance is dependent on the actual sizes of the previous time periods' error terms. It also presumes that these error terms are normally distributed, which may not always hold true in real-world data, making it important to test these assumptions prior to applying the model.

The ARCH model is mostly employed in two areas in financial markets: risk management and derivative pricing. It aids in forecasting return volatility, which is crucial for risk measures like Value at Risk (VaR). In derivative pricing, the ARCH model helps price options and other derivatives sensitive to the underlying asset's volatility.

The ARCH model's capability to assess volatility over time makes it particularly beneficial for financial analysts and investors. It aids them in understanding the potential risks associated with their investment decisions, especially in volatile markets. By offering insights into potential future price variations, the ARCH model can assist investors in making better-informed decisions.

However, the ARCH model has its limitations. It assumes that shocks are symmetric, meaning that positive and negative shocks have the same effect on volatility, which is often not the case in financial markets. To address this, the Generalized Autoregressive Conditional Heteroskedasticity (GARCH) model was developed to allow past variances to influence current variance, capturing the 'leverage effect'.

Another drawback of the ARCH model is that it may not be suitable for long-term forecasting due to being a short-term model. For long-term forecasts, other models like the stochastic volatility model may be more suitable.

Despite these shortcomings, the ARCH model remains a fundamental tool in volatility modeling due to its simplicity and easy interpretability, making it a preferred choice among financial analysts. It continues to be broadly used in a variety of financial applications, ranging from risk management to asset pricing. **This guide aims to give you a fundamental understanding of the ARCH model and how it can be utilized to forecast stock prices.**

Understanding ARCH: Prior to using the ARCH model for stock prediction, it's crucial to comprehend its concept. ARCH is a model that identifies volatility clustering, a common characteristic in financial data series. This means periods of low volatility are usually succeeded by similar periods, and the same applies to high volatility periods.

Data Collection: The initial step when using the ARCH model is to gather historical data on the stock prices of your interest. This information can be acquired from various financial data suppliers or your stock brokerage firm.

Data Processing: After data collection, it must be processed. This process involves cleaning up the data to eliminate any errors or anomalies that could distort the ARCH model results.

Choosing the Right ARCH Model: There are several ARCH model variants, such as GARCH, EGARCH, and IGARCH. Each model has its pros and cons, making it essential to choose the most suitable one for your data.

Setting Up the Model: Once you've selected the appropriate ARCH model, it needs to be set up. This step requires specifying the lag length for the autoregressive and moving average components of the model.

Model Estimation: The next stage involves estimating the model parameters. This is usually achieved through maximum likelihood estimation.

Testing for ARCH Effects: After estimating the model, it's essential to test for ARCH effects. This is done by conducting a Lagrange Multiplier (LM) test. If significant ARCH effects are found, the model is considered a good fit for the data.

Making Predictions: After the ARCH model is set up and estimated, it can be used to make predictions. The model forecasts the future variance of stock prices, which can be used to predict future prices.

Interpreting the Results: Results from the ARCH model should be interpreted with care. The model predicts variance, not actual prices. Therefore, the predictions should be seen as a risk measure, not an exact forecast of future prices.

Re-Estimate the Model: The ARCH model should be re-estimated as new data becomes available to ensure its accuracy and relevance.

Using the Predictions: The ARCH model predictions can be applied in various ways, such as informing trading decisions, managing risk, or constructing portfolios.

Limitations of ARCH: While the ARCH model is a powerful tool for predicting stock price volatility, it has limitations. It assumes that volatility is time-varying and follows an autoregressive process, which may not always be true.

Combining with Other Models: The ARCH model can be combined with other models to overcome its limitations. For instance, it can be used with the Black-Scholes model for options pricing or with the Capital Asset Pricing Model (CAPM) to calculate equity cost.

Advanced Techniques: Stochastic volatility models or jump diffusion models can be explored for those interested in more advanced techniques. These models can capture more complex dynamics in stock prices.

Continued Learning: Because the field of financial econometrics is always evolving, it's crucial to stay current with the latest research and developments.

Practice: The most effective way to learn the ARCH model is through practice. Try applying the model to various stocks to see its performance.

Software: Various software programs, such as R, Python, EViews, and Stata, can help you implement the ARCH model.

Consult with Experts: If you're new to financial modeling, consider seeking advice from an expert. They can help you understand the ARCH model's intricacies and guide you through the process.

Critically Evaluate: Always critically assess the ARCH model's predictions. Remember, no model is perfect, and all predictions carry a certain level of uncertainty.

Final Thought: Despite its limitations, the ARCH model is a potent tool for predicting stock price volatility. When used correctly, it can provide valuable insights and inform investment decisions. Remember, successful investing is not just about having the right tools, but also using them effectively.

Hypothetical Situation: Visualize yourself as an investor eyeing a specific stock, for instance, Alphabet Inc., Google's parent company. You aim to predict the future fluctuations of this stock to guide your investment choices.

Actionable Approaches:

Data Gathering: Begin by amassing historical stock prices of Alphabet Inc. This information can be acquired from financial data providers or your brokerage house.

Data Handling: Purge the gathered data of any inaccuracies or discrepancies that could skew the model's outcomes.

Model Selection: Considering the data's characteristics, you may find the GARCH model (a derivative of the ARCH model) appropriate as it takes into account past variances and past errors.

Model Configuration: Configure the GARCH model by defining the lag length for the autoregressive and moving average elements.

Model Calculation: Employ the maximum likelihood estimation method to calculate the model parameters.

ARCH Effects Testing: Execute a Lagrange Multiplier (LM) test to verify significant ARCH effects. If detected, it signifies the model is well-suited for your data.

Forecasting: Use the GARCH model to predict the future fluctuation of Alphabet Inc.'s stock prices.

Results Interpretation: Keep in mind that the model is forecasting volatility, not exact prices. Utilize this as a risk measurement.

Model Re-estimation: When new data emerges, re-calculate the model to ensure its precision.

Application of Predictions: These forecasts can guide your trading decisions. For example, if the predicted volatility is high, you might choose to postpone buying the stock until it stabilizes.

Integration with Other Models: To estimate the potential return on your investment, think about using the GARCH model along with the Capital Asset Pricing Model (CAPM).

Expert Consultation: If any part of this process is unclear, seek advice from a financial advisor or a professional skilled in financial econometrics.

Critical Assessment: Always scrutinize the predictions. Bear in mind that all models have limitations and there's always a degree of uncertainty with any forecast.

By implementing these methods, you can practically apply the ARCH model in real-time to anticipate stock price volatility and make well-informed investment choices.

Here's an example of how the prediction process works using past data of Alphabet Inc.'s stock prices over five years. After cleaning the data and choosing the GARCH model for analysis, we'll say the lag length has been set to 1 for both the autoregressive and moving average parts. Following the calculation of the model parameters using the maximum likelihood estimation method, the ARCH effect proves significant, validating the suitability of the GARCH model for your data.

Suppose the model predicts a high level of volatility for the upcoming trading day. This doesn't provide an exact price, but indicates a potential for significant price fluctuation. As an investor, understanding this could be seen as high risk, and you might decide to pause on purchasing the stock.

In terms of calculating possible returns, the GARCH model can be combined with the Capital Asset Pricing Model (CAPM). Let's say the anticipated return of Alphabet Inc. using CAPM is calculated to be 10%. However, considering the high volatility predicted by the GARCH model, you might conclude that the potential 10% return doesn't outweigh the risk.

We'll use Alphabet Inc. as a case study, presuming that the company's stock has experienced an average return of 8% over the previous five years. The risk-free rate stands at 2%, with the anticipated market return at 7%. The CAPM model can be employed to predict the stock's expected return.

Firstly, the stock's beta, which gauges the stock's market volatility, needs to be calculated. Let's assume Alphabet Inc.'s beta is 1.2. The CAPM formula is as follows: Expected return = Risk-free rate + Beta (Market return - Risk-free rate). Substituting the values, we find: Expected return = 2% + 1.2 (7% - 2%) = 8%. This implies that Alphabet Inc.'s stock's expected return is 8%, aligning with the historical average.

Moving forward, let's say that the GARCH model forecasts a high volatility level for Alphabet Inc.'s stock in the next trading day, signifying a considerable possibility of the stock's return deviating from the 8% expected return.

Assuming the GARCH model predicts a 20% stock volatility, this implies that the stock's return could change by 20% in either direction. Hence, the stock's return could range from -12% to 28% (8% - 20% to 8% + 20%).

As an investor, you have to determine whether the possible 28% return justifies the risk of a -12% return. If you're risk-averse, you might conclude that the potential 10% return (from the CAPM model) doesn't compensate for the risk of a -12% return (from the GARCH model), and decide against investing in the stock.

Please note, this is a simplified scenario and various other factors would also require consideration when making investment decisions. Additionally, both the GARCH and CAPM models have their limitations and should not be the only basis for investment decisions.

Extreme Value Theory (EVT)

Extreme Value Theory (EVT) is a probability model often employed for evaluating stock prices in the financial sector. This theory is particularly effective for modeling and measuring extreme events or outliers that significantly influence the stock market. These events tend to surpass the range of typical fluctuations and are recognized by their severity and rarity. EVT investigates the behavior of extreme outliers and risks related to tail events. The theory is grounded on the idea that only the most extreme values significantly influence the overall risk. Consequently, it concentrates on understanding the behavior of extreme events, which could be a rapid surge or drop in stock prices.

The application of EVT in the stock market is critical, especially for risk management and financial decision-making. It assists investors and traders in estimating the likelihood of extreme stock price changes, assessing potential losses, and making knowledgeable decisions. It is particularly valuable during times of economic instability or financial crises when stock prices can vary drastically.

EVT offers a mathematical method for evaluating extreme events. It employs statistical methods to model and predict the occurrence of extreme events. These models are crucial for calculating the risk associated with rare events that could potentially result in significant losses in the financial market. EVT models are frequently used alongside other financial models to provide a more thorough assessment of market risk. For example, they can be combined with Value at Risk (VaR) models, which estimate the potential loss in value of a risky asset or portfolio over a specified period for a given confidence interval. However, traditional VaR models often fall short in accurately predicting losses during extreme market events. This is where EVT proves its worth. It enhances the accuracy of VaR models by accurately modeling and predicting extreme events, thus offering a more reliable measure of market risk.

The use of EVT is not restricted to risk management. It's also employed in portfolio optimization, financial regulation, and insurance. By accurately predicting extreme events, EVT assists in optimizing asset distribution in a portfolio, ensuring regulatory compliance in financial markets, and pricing insurance products.

EVT models are particularly helpful in evaluating the risk of fat-tailed distributions, which are commonly seen in financial returns. Fat tails suggest a higher likelihood of extreme events happening than what is anticipated by the normal distribution, frequently used in financial modeling.

Several techniques have been created within the EVT framework for modeling stock prices. One such technique is the Peaks Over Threshold (POT) method, which focuses on exceedances over a certain threshold. Another method is the Block Maxima (BM) method, which focuses on the maximum values within equally-sized blocks of a time series.

Despite its many benefits, EVT also has specific limitations. Most importantly, it requires a large data set for accurate modeling, especially for very extreme events. Additionally, EVT models assume that extreme events are independent of each other, which may not always be the case in the financial market.

EVT also necessitates careful choice of the threshold value. If the threshold is set too low, the model may include too many non-extreme values, resulting in inaccurate results. Conversely, if the threshold is set too high, the model may lack enough data for accurate modeling.

Extreme Value Theory (EVT) is a statistical approach that concentrates on severe deviations from the median of probability distributions. In the stock market, EVT is applied to forecast and manage the risks involved with drastic market fluctuations like crashes or sudden share price increases. This is a practical guide on how to utilize EVT in predicting stock market prices.

Firstly, it's crucial to understand that EVT is grounded in the statistical analysis of extreme values, as opposed to average or typical values. Within the stock market, this implies that EVT targets the highest or lowest share prices, often resulting from rare and extreme events.

The initial step in utilizing EVT to predict share prices requires gathering historical data on these prices. This data should encompass not just the usual highs and lows, but also the exceptionally high and low prices. The larger the data pool, the more precise your predictions will be.

Upon gathering the necessary data, the next step involves fitting this data into an extreme value distribution, a statistical distribution that models the probabilities of extreme events. Several types of extreme value distributions exist, such as the Gumbel, Frechet, and Weibull distributions.

After fitting your data into an extreme value distribution, you can apply this model to forecast the likelihood of future extreme events. For example, if your model indicates a high likelihood of a drastic drop in share prices, you may want to consider selling your shares ahead of this event.

It's worth noting that EVT is not a guaranteed method for predicting share prices. Like all statistical models, it's based on certain assumptions and can only forecast probabilities, not certainties. However, by concentrating on extreme events, EVT offers a unique insight into market risks that other models may overlook.

A significant advantage of EVT is its ability to assist investors and traders in managing their risks. By forecasting the likelihood of extreme market events, EVT can provide early warnings of potential crashes or share price spikes. This enables investors and traders to take preventative action, such as diversifying their portfolio or setting stop-loss orders.

However, remember that EVT doesn't just predict negative events. It can also forecast the likelihood of exceptionally high share prices, which can present profitable opportunities. By identifying these potential opportunities, EVT can help investors and traders maximize their returns.

Another crucial aspect of EVT is the notion of tail dependence, which relates to the correlation between extreme events in different stocks or markets. By examining this correlation, EVT can help predict the effect of an extreme event in one market on other markets.

Assume you're a tech industry investor with substantial investments in several tech companies, and you're keen to forecast extreme events in this sector. You would use Extreme Value Theory (EVT) by initially gathering historical data on your tech stocks' share prices. This data should encompass not just average highs and lows but also any major surges or plunges in share prices. You can obtain this data from financial websites or databases, or automate the process with a data scraping tool.

After gathering your data, you would then fit it into an extreme value distribution like the Gumbel, Frechet, or Weibull distribution. You could accomplish this with statistical software or programming languages such as R or Python.

Once your model is established, you can use it to anticipate the probability of future extreme events in the tech industry. For instance, if your model shows a high chance of a considerable decrease in tech share prices, you might opt to sell some of your tech stocks or diversify into other sectors.

On the other hand, if your model forecasts a high possibility of a significant rise in tech share prices, you may choose to buy more tech stocks or maintain your current ones. You could also use this insight to set stop-loss orders, which would sell your stocks automatically if their prices dip below a certain threshold.

Moreover, by studying the tail dependence between your tech stocks and other markets, you could foresee how a tech industry extreme event might impact your other investments. For example, if your model reveals a strong correlation between tech stocks and the general stock market, you might brace for a wider market decline in the case of a tech crash.

To demonstrate the application of Extreme Value Theory (EVT) in predicting stock market prices, let's take a hypothetical situation involving a single tech stock. Let's say you have a decade's worth of historical data on the tech stock's daily returns. You notice that these daily returns typically follow a normal distribution, but sometimes there are unusually high or low returns.

In using EVT, the first step would be to identify these abnormal events by setting a return threshold considerably higher or lower than the average return. For example, if the average daily return of the stock is 1%, you may set the threshold at 5% to focus only on the most extreme events.

Next, you would use EVT to analyze the returns that surpass this threshold, fitting them into an extreme value distribution like the Gumbel, Frechet, or Weibull distribution. You might discover, for instance, that these extreme returns align with a Frechet distribution with a shape parameter of 0.2 and a scale parameter of 3%.

Having developed a model for the stock's extreme returns, you can calculate the likelihood of future extreme events. You might want to know the probability of the stock's return falling below -10% in a single day. Your model may predict this probability to be, for instance, 0.01, or 1%.

In this manner, EVT can help predict the probability of significant fluctuations in the stock's price, assisting in making investment decisions. For instance, if the risk of a significant decrease in the stock's price is too high, you might choose to sell the stock or place a stop-loss order. On the other hand, if a substantial increase in the stock's price is probable, you might consider buying more of the stock.

144

Suppose you're an investor who has been monitoring the stock of TechX, a certain tech company, for a decade. You've observed that the daily returns usually follow a normal distribution with occasional exceptionally high or low returns. You decide to use Extreme Value Theory (EVT) to study significant fluctuations in stock returns. For example, the stock's average daily return is 1%, but there have been days with returns as high as 10% or as low as -10%. You set a 5% threshold to concentrate on the most extreme events.

You have a dataset of 2,500 trading days (roughly 10 years' worth of data), with 50 days showing returns exceeding 5% in either direction. These are the 'extreme' days you'll be focusing on. You then fit these 50 extreme returns into a Gumbel distribution using statistical software, resulting in a shape parameter of 0.15 and a scale parameter of 2%.

You then use this model to estimate the likelihood of future extreme events, such as the probability of the stock's return dropping below -10% on any given day. To do this, you integrate the Gumbel distribution from -10% to infinity, using the shape and scale parameters, resulting in a probability of roughly 0.02 or 2%. According to your EVT model, this means there's a 2% chance the stock's return will drop below -10% on any given day. As an investor, this information allows you to manage your risk. For example, if you believe a 2% chance of a -10% return is too high a risk, you might contemplate selling some of your TechX stocks or broadening your portfolio. Conversely, if you're comfortable with this level of risk, you might choose to retain your stocks or even purchase more.

Bear in mind that EVT offers a probability, not a certainty. While it can assist you in understanding and managing risk, it doesn't guarantee specific outcomes. Therefore, it's crucial to use EVT alongside other investment strategies and tools.

Time Series Forecasting Models

Probabilistic models are heavily relied upon in the financial sector, particularly for predicting future stock prices. These models use past data and statistical methods to make predictions about future events. Numerous probabilistic models are available, each best suited to a particular task.

One of the most commonly used models in finance is time-series forecasting models, which predict future outcomes based on past trends and behaviors. Models such as ARIMA, SARIMA, and Vector Autoregressive Models are all types of time-series models.

ARIMA (AutoRegressive Integrated Moving Average) is a forecasting method that uses historical data to predict future values. It is particularly effective for datasets that exhibit trends or seasonal patterns. The model takes into account three components: the difference between observations (integrated), the weighted average of past observations (autoregressive), and the weighted average of past forecast errors (moving average).

SARIMA (Seasonal AutoRegressive Integrated Moving Average) is another widely used forecasting method for time-series data, particularly for data that demonstrates seasonal trends. It adds an additional parameter to the ARIMA model to account for seasonality.

Vector autoregressive (VAR) models are a form of time-series model that predicts future values of multiple variables based on their past values. This model is particularly useful in predicting stock market prices, where multiple factors often influence stock prices.

The GARCH (Generalized Autoregressive Conditional Heteroskedasticity) model is also frequently used in stock price prediction. It is a statistical model for time-series data that measures variability over time and is typically used to estimate the volatility of returns for stocks, bonds, and market indices.

The Hidden Markov Model (HMM) is another probabilistic model used to forecast stock market prices. This model assumes that the system being modeled is a Markov process with hidden parameters, and the challenge lies in determining these hidden parameters from observable ones.

Other types of probabilistic models include Monte Carlo simulations, Bayesian networks, and stochastic volatility models. The choice of model depends on the nature of the stock price data, market conditions, and the forecasting needs of the investor or trader.

Monte Carlo simulations model the likelihood of different outcomes in a process that cannot be easily predicted due to random variables. Bayesian networks are probabilistic graphical models that use Bayesian inference for probability computations, aiming to model conditional dependence and causation. Stochastic volatility models, on the other hand, are used to model time series data, exhibiting random volatility over time, which is especially useful in the stock market.

Time series forecasting models are robust analytical instruments utilized in diverse sectors such as finance, economics, and business. They scrutinize past data to uncover patterns and trends, which aid in predicting future outcomes. In relation to the stock market, these models can help forecast share prices, critical information for investors and traders.

The initial step in deploying time series forecasting models to predict share prices is data collection. Typical data in this scenario include historical share prices, trading volumes, and other market indicators. Gathering ample, high-quality data is key to enhancing the accuracy of the prediction.

After data collection, the subsequent step is data cleaning and preprocessing. This entails eliminating any errors or inconsistencies in the data, dealing with missing values, and normalizing the data if required. This step is vital to guarantee that the model is trained on precise and trustworthy data.

Next, selecting the appropriate time series forecasting model is necessary. Several models are available, including Autoregressive Integrated Moving Average (ARIMA), Exponential Smoothing, and Long Short-Term Memory (LSTM) models. The choice of model hinges on the data's nature and the task's specific needs. For example, ARIMA models are appropriate for data that display a clear trend or seasonality. They capture these patterns using a blend of autoregressive (AR) and moving average (MA) terms. The 'Integrated' in ARIMA refers to differencing, a method used to make the data stationary, i.e., to eliminate trends and seasonality.

Conversely, Exponential Smoothing models are a group of forecasting methods that utilize weighted averages of past observations to predict future values. They are especially effective when the data has a clear trend or seasonal pattern.

LSTM models, a kind of recurrent neural network (RNN), are adept at learning long-term dependencies, making them particularly suitable for time series forecasting. They can handle vast amounts of data and intricate patterns, making them a favorite choice for stock price prediction.

After selecting the model, the next action is to train it on the data. This entails feeding the model with the historical data and allowing it to learn the underlying patterns and relationships. The model's performance is then assessed using a validation set, a subset of the data unseen during training.

It's crucial to fine-tune the model's parameters to enhance its performance. Methods like grid search or random search can be used, which systematically explore different parameter combinations to find the best one. The parameters of a time series forecasting model usually include the number of past observations to consider (lag), the degree of differencing, and the number of forecast steps.

Once the model is trained and tuned, it can be deployed to make predictions. In the context of stock market prediction, this would entail feeding the model with the latest share prices and market indicators and instructing it to predict future share prices.

However, remember that stock prices are influenced by numerous factors, many of which are not captured by historical data. These include macroeconomic indicators, company news, geopolitical events, and investor sentiment. Thus, the predictions made by time series forecasting models should be viewed as a guide, not a definitive prediction.

Additionally, the model's prediction accuracy should be regularly evaluated, and the model should be retrained as needed. This is because the stock market is dynamic and constantly changing, and a model that performed well in the past may not necessarily perform well in the future.

Scenario:

Let's take a real-world example of a firm in the financial services industry, FinanceCo. FinanceCo specializes in providing investment guidelines and managing portfolios for its clientele. To offer precise and current advice, it is essential for the firm to forecast future stock prices of multiple companies.

Application:

Data Collection: FinanceCo gathers historical data of diverse stocks from various sectors. This data consists of past share prices, trading volumes, and other market indicators like dividend yields, Price/Earnings ratios, and so on.

Data Cleaning and Preprocessing: FinanceCo's analysts cleanse the data by removing errors and discrepancies. They manage missing values through imputation techniques and standardize the data to maintain consistency.

Model Selection: The analysts select an appropriate model based on the data type and the specific task requirements. For data exhibiting evident trends and seasonality, they might use ARIMA.

Exponential Smoothing models may be utilized if the data contains weighted averages of past observations. LSTM models could be an ideal match for data with intricate patterns and large volumes.

Model Training: The chosen model is then trained using the historical data, enabling it to understand the inherent patterns and relationships.

Model Tuning: The analysts then adjust the model parameters to improve its performance using techniques like grid search or random search.

Forecasting: After the model has been trained and fine-tuned, it is ready to generate forecasts. Analysts input the model with the most recent share prices and market indicators and direct it to forecast future stock prices.

Strategies for Real-time Application:

Continuous Learning: Given the stock market's dynamic nature, the models should be consistently trained and updated with the most recent data to retain their forecasting accuracy.

Multi-Factor Analysis: Besides the model's predictions, analysts should also take into account other elements such as macroeconomic indicators, company updates, geopolitical events, and investor sentiment which can affect stock prices.

Risk Management: The forecasts generated by these models should be used as a reference, not as an absolute prediction. Analysts should always account for potential risks and uncertainties in the stock market.

Performance Assessment: Regularly review the model's forecasting accuracy and retrain the model when necessary. This will ensure the model's dependability over time.

By following these steps and strategies, FinanceCo can successfully forecast future share prices and offer valuable investment advice to its clients.

Several computations can be utilized to comprehend the likelihood of predicting stock market prices. For instance, the expected return on an investment is a crucial calculation in finance and can be determined using the formula:

Expected Return = Sum of (Probability of each outcome * Corresponding return of that outcome)

Let's assume that FinanceCo analysts have forecasted three potential outcomes for a specific stock over the next year based on their model:

There's a 40% chance the stock price could rise by 15%.
There's a 30% chance the stock price could rise by 10%.
There's a 30% chance the stock price could decrease by 5%.

The expected return would then be calculated as follows:

Expected Return = $(0.4 \times 15) + (0.3 \times 10) + (0.3*-5) = 6 + 3 - 1.5 = 7.5\%$

This simplified computation provides analysts with a measurable and testable forecast about future stock prices. They can contrast this prediction with the actual return and refine their model as needed, thereby increasing its predictive accuracy over time. For a more advanced model like ARIMA or LSTM, the model would account for additional factors and more intricate relationships, but the basic concept remains the same: the model generates predictions, and analysts contrast these predictions with actual results to enhance the model's precision.

Probit Models

Probabilistic models play a crucial role in financial market analysis, offering a mathematical structure that aids investors in making educated choices about asset prices. One such commonly employed model in the finance industry is the Probit Model. This is a regression type where the dependent variable can only take two values, such as Yes or No. The name Probit comes from combining probability and unit.

The Probit Model is favored for its capacity to manage dichotomous dependent variables, like stock prices rising (1) or falling (0). This model enables the prediction of the likelihood of an event happening based on a set of inputs, and it allows for the assessment of the effect of different variables on that event's occurrence.

When it comes to predicting stock prices, the Probit Model can be used to evaluate the influence of various factors on stock price fluctuations. For example, it can examine how shifts in interest rates, inflation rates, or corporate earnings may impact a stock's price. This knowledge can be useful for investors who want to safeguard their investments or capitalize on price changes.

The Probit model varies from other models like the logit model due to its assumptions about the error distribution. In a Probit model, it is assumed that the errors follow a standard normal distribution, which is ideal for financial data that often shows characteristics of normal distributions, such as symmetry and a peak at the mean.

One of the key benefits of the Probit model is its adaptability. Unlike linear regression models that assume a steady rate of change in the dependent variable for a unit change in the predictor, the Probit model allows the probability of the event's occurrence to change with different predictor levels. This is particularly beneficial in predicting stock prices, where the impact of predictor variables can greatly vary based on their levels.

However, the Probit model has its shortcomings. It requires a larger sample size to achieve the same statistical power as other models. Additionally, its results can be more difficult to understand, as the coefficients indicate changes in the z-score rather than the probability itself.

Despite these potential downsides, the Probit model remains an effective tool for financial analysts due to its ability to handle binary outcomes and its adaptability in modeling variable relationships, making it ideal for predicting stock price changes. The accuracy of the Probit model's predictions is dependent on the quality of the input data, so it is crucial for analysts to ensure their data is trustworthy and accurately represents the market conditions they are trying to forecast.

The subsequent instructions will guide you on how to utilize a probit model to forecast stock market share prices. Your initial step in applying the probit model is to compile your data. This data should include historical share prices of the company you're interested in and other pertinent details such as the company's earnings reports, industry trends, and economic indicators. This information can typically be found on financial websites or from a financial adviser.

The following step is to identify your dependent and independent variables. The share price is the dependent variable, while the independent variables are the other factors you're taking into account. For instance, you may include the company's earnings per share, the overall economy status, etc.

After you have collected your data and established your variables, you need to transform your dependent variable (share price) into a binary outcome. This is necessary as the probit model is made to forecast binary outcomes. You could label share prices as either "high" (above a particular threshold) or "low" (below a specific threshold).

You're now prepared to create your probit model. This involves utilizing a statistical software package to perform a probit regression analysis. You input your dependent and independent variables, and the software will generate the model.

The probit model's output includes coefficients for each independent variable, illustrating the relationship between each variable and the probability of the share price being high or low. For instance, a positive coefficient shows that as the variable rises, the probability of the share price being high also increases.

To apply the probit model for predicting future share prices, you must input the present values of your independent variables into the model. The model will then provide a probability of the share price being high or low.

Bear in mind that the probit model is a predictive tool and may not always be 100% accurate. It assumes the relationship between your variables and the share price will remain consistent in the future as it has been in the past. If this assumption is not accurate, the model's predictions may be off.

The probit model is also sensitive to the threshold choice for defining high and low share prices. If your threshold is too high or too low, your model may not precisely predict share prices. Additionally, the probit model can be influenced by outliers in your data. If your data contains unusually high or low values that do not reflect the typical relationship between your variables and the share price, these outliers can skew the model's predictions. Nevertheless, the probit model can be a handy tool for forecasting share prices. By considering a range of factors and their relationship to the share price, the probit model can offer a more sophisticated prediction than simply examining past share prices.

To effectively utilize the probit model, it is crucial to regularly update your model with fresh data. As new financial reports are released and as the economy fluctuates, you should include this new information into your model.

When used appropriately, the probit model can assist you in making more educated decisions about buying and selling stocks. By predicting the possibility of a stock's price rising or falling, you can better evaluate the risk and reward of various investment options.

Lastly, while the probit model can be a worthy tool, it should not be the sole factor you rely on when making investment decisions. It's always vital to consider a variety of factors and to seek advice from a financial advisor if you're uncertain.

Hypothetical Situation:

Assume you're an investor looking to buy shares from a tech company called TechX. You choose to use the probit model to anticipate the future stock prices of TechX. You gather historical data on TechX's stock prices, earnings per share, and trends in the tech sector. You also collect data on macroeconomic indicators such as inflation rates and GDP growth.

The stock price is your dependent variable, while earnings per share, tech market trends, and the economic indicators act as your independent variables. You then convert the stock price into a binary outcome, labeling them as "high" if they exceed a certain limit, say $100, and "low" if they fall below this limit.

You conduct a probit regression analysis using a statistical software package, inputting the stock prices (now in binary format) and the independent variables. The software provides a model with coefficients for each independent variable, indicating how each factor affects the likelihood of the stock price being high or low. For instance, if the coefficient for TechX's earnings per share is positive, it suggests that an increase in TechX's earnings per share raises the likelihood of the stock price being high. **Practical Approaches:** Continuously update the model: With the release of new financial reports from TechX or changes in macroeconomic conditions, you should refresh the model with this new data to ensure its accuracy. Be vigilant for outliers: Keep an eye out for extremely high or low values in your data that could distort the model's forecasts. You may need to modify your model or further investigate these outliers. Treat the model as a guide, not a certainty: Keep in mind, the probit model offers probabilities, not guarantees. Use the model's forecasts as part of your decision-making process but also take into account other factors like your risk tolerance, investment objectives, and advice from financial advisors. Check the model's assumptions: If you observe that the relationships between your variables and the stock price are shifting, it might be time to reassess the model's assumptions and make necessary adjustments.

Let's consider the following historical data we've gathered for TechX:

Earnings per share (EPS): $5

Tech market trend: Exhibiting a 10% growth

Inflation Rate: 2%

GDP Growth: 3%

The probit model has generated these coefficients:

Coefficient for EPS: 0.6

Coefficient for tech market trend: 0.3

Coefficient for inflation rate: -0.2

Coefficient for GDP growth: 0.1

We can use these coefficients to compute the z-score, which is integral to the probit model.

The z-score is computed using the formula:

$z = 0.6(\text{EPS}) + 0.3(\text{Tech market trend}) - 0.2(\text{Inflation rate}) + 0.1(\text{GDP Growth})$. Substituting our data into the formula gives:

$z = 0.6 \times 5 + 0.3 \times 10 - 0.2 \times 2 + 0.1 \times 3 = 6$

This z-score is then used to determine the probability from the standard normal distribution table. With a z-score of 6, which is extremely high, it signifies a very high probability (almost 1, or 100%) that the price will exceed $100.

Hence, based on this probit model, our forecast is that it's highly probable that TechX's stock price will remain high.

Latent Dirichlet Allocation (LDA)

Analyzing stock prices in the stock market is a challenging task that necessitates the use of advanced and efficient probabilistic models. The Latent Dirichlet Allocation (LDA) is one such model that has demonstrated its effectiveness in assessing and predicting stock prices.

LDA is a generative statistical model that enables sets of observations to be elucidated by unseen groups. These invisible groups assist in understanding why certain parts of the data are alike. This model is especially beneficial in the stock market context as it aids in uncovering patterns and trends that aren't immediately visible through conventional analysis methods.

In the context of the stock market, LDA can categorize similar stocks based on their historical performance. This can reveal market trends and patterns and can be utilized to forecast future performance. As an illustration, if a certain group of stocks has consistently done well in the past, there's a likelihood of them continuing to perform well in the future.

Moreover, LDA can also help in spotting underlying factors that affect stock prices. These factors can encompass various macroeconomic indicators, company-specific news, or fluctuations in market sentiment. By pinpointing these factors, investors can acquire a better comprehension of what drives stock prices, thereby making more enlightened investment choices.

An additional benefit of employing LDA in the stock market is its ability to diminish the dimensionality of the data. In essence, it helps simplify the data by concentrating on the most crucial factors, making the data more manageable to analyze and potentially enhancing the precision of predictions.

However, it's important to note that LDA, while a strong tool for analyzing stock prices, has its restrictions. One of the main constraints of LDA is its assumption that the factors influencing stock prices are independent of each other. This is not always the case in reality, as various factors often interact with each other in intricate ways.

Moreover, LDA also presumes that the distribution of topics in each document (in this instance, the distribution of factors affecting each stock's price) is Dirichlet. This implies a specific form for this distribution, which may not always be precise.

Despite these constraints, LDA continues to be a valuable tool in the analysis of stock prices. By assisting in identifying patterns and trends in the market, and simplifying data, LDA can help investors make more informed choices and potentially lead to better investment results.

This guide aspires to outline how this could be implemented.

Understanding LDA and its functioning is key. LDA is a probabilistic model that presumes each document (for instance, a company's financial report or news article) is a blend of a specific number of topics, with each topic represented by a distribution of words. The aim is to categorize the documents into these topics based on their content.

To utilize LDA in the stock market, it's important to gather relevant textual data like financial news or company reports that could influence stock prices. These documents can then be analyzed using LDA to pinpoint the main topics being discussed.

After the data collection and preprocessing (which includes cleaning, tokenizing, and vectorizing the text), we apply the LDA model. This is achieved by defining the number of topics we want the model to identify and then educating the model with our preprocessed data.

The result of the LDA model is an assortment of topics, each characterized by a distribution of words. These topics can be interpreted by examining the words with the highest probabilities within each topic. For instance, a topic with words like 'dividend', 'profit', and 'revenue' likely pertains to financial performance.

The crucial step now is to associate these topics with stock price fluctuations. This can be achieved by monitoring the frequency of these topics over time and linking it with changes in stock prices.

For example, if a financial performance-related topic becomes more prevalent, we might anticipate a rise in the stock price.

The subsequent step is to design a predictive model, potentially a machine learning model that uses the topic distributions as input and predicts future stock price movements. This model must be trained on historical data, and its effectiveness should be appraised on a separate validation set to avoid overfitting.

One significant factor to consider when designing the predictive model is feature selection. Not all topics identified by LDA may be pertinent for predicting stock prices. Some topics may create noise and could deteriorate the model's performance, so careful feature selection is vital.

Another consideration is data timeliness. Stock prices are highly responsive to the most recent information. Hence, the model needs regular updates with the latest data to preserve its predictive capacity.

Due to the complexity of the stock market, a single model may not suffice. Merging the LDA-based model with other data-driven models (like technical indicators or macroeconomic data) may enhance the overall predictive ability.

Hypothetical Case Study:

Consider this situation. We want to predict the future stock prices of the tech behemoth, Apple Inc. We begin by collecting pertinent text-based data about the company. This could encompass financial reports, press releases, news articles, etc., sourced from credible platforms.

Step 1: Gathering Data

We could employ web scraping methods to compile this data from financial news sites, the official Apple website, news aggregators, etc.

Step 2: Data Preprocessing

The gathered data is then cleaned. We remove irrelevant content, punctuation, special characters, and tokenize the text. The text is then converted into a matrix of token counts, a process known as vectorization.

Step 3: Implementing LDA

We apply the LDA model, under the assumption that each document is a combination of a certain number of topics. We decide the number of topics we want the model to recognize, for example, we might opt for 5 topics.

Step 4: Topic Interpretation

The output from the LDA model will be these 5 topics, each represented by a distribution of words. A topic with words like 'innovation', 'patent', 'technology', likely relates to Apple's technological advancements.

Step 5: Linking Topics with Stock Prices

The subsequent step is to determine whether the occurrence of these topics over time correlates with Apple's stock prices. Techniques such as regression analysis or time series analysis could be used for this purpose.

Step 6: Creating a Predictive Model

We can then develop a machine learning model that uses these topic distributions as input to predict future stock price movements. This model would be trained on historical data and validated on a separate dataset.

Step 7: Feature Selection and Regular Updates
It's important to ensure that the selected features are relevant for predicting stock prices. It's also crucial to keep the model updated with the latest data to maintain its predictive accuracy.

Step 8: Merging Models
The LDA-based model could be combined with other data-driven models to improve prediction accuracy. For example, we could include technical indicators like moving averages or MACD, or macroeconomic data such as GDP growth rate, inflation rate, etc.

Real-time Application:
The developed predictive system could be used in real time to anticipate Apple's stock price movements. This would assist investors in making informed decisions about when to buy or sell Apple's stock, potentially leading to increased profits.

To keep things simple, let's imagine we've already run our LDA model and identified five topics that seem to be linked with Apple's stock prices: Product Launches, Technological Innovation, Financial Performance, Market Trends, and Legal Issues. We can then assign probabilities to each subject based on their frequency in the text data. For instance, Product Launches might be at 30%, Technological Innovation at 25%, and so on.

The next step would be to use regression analysis to determine the correlation between these subjects and Apple's stock prices. Let's hypothesize that we find the following correlations: Product Launches with 0.80, Technological Innovation with 0.75, and so forth.

These probabilities and correlations can then be used to forecast stock prices. For example, a spike in articles about 'Technological Innovation' (rising from 25% to 35%) may lead to a positive effect on the stock prices, considering its positive correlation of 0.75.

On the other hand, if articles about 'Legal Issues' increase (from 10% to 20%), we could foresee a possible negative impact on the stock prices due to its lower positive correlation of 0.60.

Remember, this is a simplified scenario. In real-life situations, more complex models would be used and other factors such as market sentiment and investor behavior would also be taken into account. Additionally, regular model updates with the latest data would be crucial to maintain its predictive accuracy.

Let's create an easy-to-understand example that shows how we can use topic probabilities and their relationship with stock prices to predict future changes in the stock market.

Consider a single corporation, for instance, Apple Inc. Let's say we've run our LDA model on a collection of text data related to Apple and identified five topics. Each of these topics is given a probability based on their frequency within the text data:

Product Launches: 30%

Technological Innovation: 25%

Financial Performance: 20%

Market Trends: 15%

Legal Issues: 10%

Next, we apply regression analysis to identify relationships between these topics and Apple's stock prices, yielding the following correlations:

Product Launches: 0.80

Technological Innovation: 0.75

Financial Performance: 0.70

Market Trends: 0.65

Legal Issues: -0.60

The negative correlation for Legal Issues suggests that an increase in this topic could cause a decrease in Apple's stock price.

To predict the impact of these topics on Apple's stock price, we can compute a weighted average of the topic probabilities, using their correlations as weights.

Weighted Average = sum of (Topic Probability * Topic Correlation)

$$= (0.30 \times 0.80) + (0.25 \times 0.75) + (0.20 \times 0.70) + (0.15 \times 0.65) + (0.10 * -0.60)$$

$$= 0.605$$

This weighted average can be viewed as a broad measure of the expected change in Apple's stock price given the current topic distribution.

Now, let's say there's a sudden increase in articles about 'Technological Innovation', and its probability rises from 25% to 35%. Keeping all other topic probabilities the same, the new weighted average would be:

New Weighted Average = $(0.30 \times 0.80) + (0.35 \times 0.75) + (0.20 \times 0.70) + (0.15 \times 0.65) + (0.10 * -0.60) = 0.68$

The rise in the weighted average from 0.605 to 0.68 suggests a probable increase in Apple's stock price given the increased focus on 'Technological Innovation'.

Gaussian Mixture Models (GMM)

Financial analysis increasingly relies on probabilistic models, notably for forecasting stock market prices. The Gaussian Mixture Model (GMM) is a particularly prevalent tool used in this field. This article aims to provide an understanding of GMM's role, importance, and usage within financial markets.

The GMM is a probabilistic model that merges various Gaussian distributions to deliver a more adaptable probability distribution model. It is particularly effective in complex financial data analysis, as it can identify detailed and subtle aspects usually missed by more basic models.

GMMs are sophisticated in their ability to model multiple distributions simultaneously. This is particularly beneficial when analyzing stock prices, which often follow a non-linear distribution due to various influencing factors such as investor sentiment, economic indicators, and company performance.

In terms of stock prices, a single Gaussian distribution may not adequately capture the market's complexity and volatility. This is where the GMM proves useful. It enables the modeling of stock price behavior as a blend of several Gaussian distributions, each representing different market states.

The application of GMM in the stock market starts with determining the number of Gaussian distributions to use. This is usually accomplished using a process called Expectation-Maximization (EM), a statistical method that estimates the GMM parameters in an iterative process to maximize the observed data's likelihood.

Once the Gaussian distributions are established, each is allocated a weight, which reflects its contribution to the overall model. This weight is based on the probability that a specific stock price originates from that particular distribution. This process enables the GMM to better capture the diversity of stock market movements.

The parameters of these distributions, including their means and variances, provide valuable insights into stock price behavior. For example, a distribution's mean could represent a specific market state, such as a bullish or bearish phase, while the variance could signal price volatility during that phase.

One significant benefit of using GMMs in stock price forecasting is their adaptability. They are not limited to a particular form or structure, enabling them to adjust to the stock market's dynamic nature. They can manage both symmetric and asymmetric data, account for outliers, and deal with multiple modes in the data distribution.

However, GMMs do have their limitations. They require ample high-quality data to perform effectively and can be computationally heavy, especially for high-dimensional data. Despite these issues, their capacity to capture the complexity and volatility of stock prices makes them a valuable financial analysis tool.

Further, the GMM's probabilistic nature allows it to quantify prediction uncertainty, which is crucial in the inherently uncertain field of stock price prediction. This enables investors and analysts to make informed decisions by providing a measure of the risk associated with a particular stock.

This idea can be applied in predicting stock market prices. To use GMM for predicting stock market prices, you would first collect historical stock market data, including opening and closing prices, the highest and lowest prices of the day, volume of stocks traded, and any other relevant data. The more data you have, the more accurate the GMM predictions will be.

Next, you would preprocess the data, which includes cleaning the data, managing missing values, and normalizing the data. Normalization ensures that all features are on the same scale, which is crucial for the GMM algorithm.

Then, you would divide the data into a training set and a testing set. The training set is used to train the GMM model, while the testing set is used to evaluate the model's performance. A common division is 80% for training and 20% for testing.

With the data prepared, you can now create the GMM model. In Python, you can use the GaussianMixture function from the sklearn.mixture library. You need to determine the number of components (i.e., the number of Gaussian distributions) in the GMM based on your understanding of the data and the problem. After the model is created, you can train it using the fit method, which uses the training data to estimate the parameters of the Gaussian distributions, including the mean and covariance of each distribution.

Once the model is trained, it can be used to make predictions using the predict method. It takes new data and returns the most likely component (i.e., Gaussian distribution) for each data point. In the context of stock market prediction, each data point could represent a specific day's features, and the prediction would represent the expected closing price for that day.

It should be noted that GMM is a probabilistic model, meaning it provides a probability distribution of possible outcomes, which can be beneficial in predicting stock market prices as it allows for quantifying prediction uncertainty.

After prediction comes evaluation, where you can compare the predicted closing prices with the actual closing prices in the testing set to gauge the model's performance. Evaluation metrics can include mean squared error or mean absolute error.

GMMs are particularly effective at modeling complex, multimodal data, making them suitable for stock market prediction because stock prices often display complex patterns that simpler models struggle to capture.

However, it's critical to remember that predicting the stock market is extremely difficult, and no model can offer perfect predictions. Even advanced models can be disrupted by unforeseen events, such as economic crises or company-specific news.

Also, GMMs can be sensitive to parameter initialization. Different initializations can result in different final models. To address this, you can run the GMM algorithm multiple times with different initializations and choose the model that performs best on the training data.

Finally, although GMMs can be a powerful tool for stock market prediction, they should not be used alone. Combining them with other models and techniques, like time series analysis or deep learning models, can help capture different data aspects and enhance overall performance.

Consider a realistic example where a financial company is looking to forecast future prices of a specific stock, for instance, Apple Inc. (AAPL). They can utilize GMM for this task in the following way:

Data Collection: The company gathers historical data on AAPL's stock prices, including daily opening and closing prices, highest and lowest prices, and the volume of stocks traded.

Data Preprocessing: The company cleans the data, handles missing values, and normalizes the data. Normalization is essential as it puts all features on an equal scale, which is vital for the GMM algorithm.

Train-Test Split: The company divides the data into a training set (80%) and a testing set (20%). The training set is for training the

GMM model, while the testing set is for evaluating the model's performance.

GMM Model Creation: The company employs the GaussianMixture function from the sklearn.mixture library in Python to develop the GMM model. They opt to use three components for the GMM, symbolizing three potential market states: bearish, neutral, and bullish.

Model Training: The company instructs the GMM model using the fit method, which calculates the parameters of the Gaussian distributions.

Prediction: The company utilizes the trained GMM model to forecast the closing prices of AAPL stock for the days in the testing set.

Evaluation: The company contrasts the predicted closing prices with the actual closing prices in the testing set to assess the model's performance. They use the mean squared error as their evaluation metric.

For real-time stock price predictions, the company would need to integrate the latest data into the model. As fresh data is received daily, the company can retrain the model or update its parameters, and then use it to predict the closing price for the following day.

Additionally, the company could execute the GMM algorithm several times with different initializations to solve the problem of parameter sensitivity and select the model that performs best on the training data.

Moreover, the company could blend the GMM with other prediction models or methods, like time series analysis or deep learning models, to improve prediction performance and capture different data aspects.

It's crucial to recognize that while GMM can offer a probabilistic distribution of potential outcomes, stock market price predictions are inherently uncertain and can be affected by a myriad of unpredictable factors. Therefore, the GMM's predictions should be used as guidance, not definitive truth.

Let's illustrate a hypothetical situation based on the above context where we aim to forecast the next day's closing price for AAPL stock by using the GMM model. Assume that the model has been trained with historical data and has identified three Gaussian distributions that represent bearish, neutral, and bullish market conditions. Each of these states is associated with a decrease, no change, or an increase in the stock price. More specifically, the model discovered that:

The bearish state corresponds to an average price decrease of $2 with a $0.5 standard deviation. The neutral state corresponds to an average price change of $0 with a $0.1 standard deviation. The bullish state corresponds to an average price increase of $2 with a $0.5 standard deviation.

Now, if the closing price of AAPL stock today was $150, the GMM model can use the Gaussian distributions' parameters to estimate the likelihood of each state occurring tomorrow. Assume the GMM model estimates these probabilities as 30% for the bearish state, 40% for the neutral state, and 30% for the bullish state.

Using these probabilities, we can compute the expected closing price for tomorrow as follows:

Expected closing price = $150 + (-$2 × 0.3) + ($0 × 0.4) + ($2 × 0.3) = $150 - $0.6 + $0 + $0.6 = $150.

Therefore, the GMM model predicts the expected closing price of AAPL stock for tomorrow to be $150. This is a simplified scenario, and the actual computation would involve more complicated mathematical operations due to Gaussian distributions' nature. The fundamental concept, however, is that the GMM model uses historical data to estimate the likelihood of various outcomes and then predicts based on these probabilities.

It's crucial to note that while this method can provide a probabilistic distribution of potential outcomes, the actual stock price can be affected by numerous unpredictable factors.

Neural Network Models

Financial markets predictions heavily depend on probabilistic models, with the Neural Network Model being one of the most frequently used for forecasting stock prices. These models, a subset of machine learning, are designed to mimic the human brain, processing large amounts of data to identify complex patterns. Neural networks contain input and output layers and usually a hidden layer that transforms the input data. They are highly effective in finding complex patterns that are too numerous or complicated for human programmers to decipher.

Neural networks' potential in the financial sector is significant, especially for predicting stock market trends. They excel at understanding and modeling complex, non-linear relationships - a common characteristic of financial markets. Unlike other predictive methods that use linear or simple non-linear functions, neural networks can handle multiple inputs and outputs simultaneously and identify intricate relationships between variables. Consequently, they are widely used in various financial applications, from forecasting to decision making.

Predictions of stock prices often combine neural network models with other technical and fundamental indicators. The final prediction value is a weighted average of these indicators and the neural network model's prediction. These models are trained with historical data and, once trained, can forecast future stock prices. Neural network models' predictive power comes from their ability to learn from historical data and predict future trends. This involves adjusting the networks' weights and biases, a process known as backpropagation. However, there are limitations to these models. They require a large volume of data for training to ensure accuracy, which can be a disadvantage for small companies or recent IPOs without extensive historical data. Additionally, they are often considered a "black box" model, accurately predicting trends but not providing insight into why a particular prediction was made. This can be problematic for investors seeking to understand the reasoning behind a stock price prediction.

Despite these challenges, the use of neural network models for stock price predictions is on the rise. Technological advancements are facilitating the gathering and processing of large data volumes, encouraging the adoption of these models.

Neural network models, inspired by the human brain and a subset of machine learning, are increasingly being applied in various sectors, including the stock market, to predict share prices. **This guide will show you how to use these models to forecast share prices.**

Understanding Neural Networks: These machine learning algorithms mimic the human brain's functions, learning and predicting patterns based on trained data. They consist of input and output layers, with hidden layers processing the inputs.

Data Collection: The initial step in using neural networks for stock price prediction involves data collection. This requires historical stock price data, obtainable from financial websites, APIs or purchasing from data providers. The data should include open, close, high, low prices and trade volumes.

Data Preprocessing: Following data collection, preprocessing is necessary. This entails data cleaning, normalization, and splitting. Cleaning involves correcting or removing erroneous data, normalization involves adjusting numeric variables to a common scale, and splitting involves dividing your dataset into training and testing sets.

Defining the Neural Network Architecture: You then define your neural network model's architecture, which includes specifying the number of layers, neurons per layer, the activation function, and other parameters. The model's complexity depends on the stock data's nature.

Training the Model: The training data is fed into the neural network model which learns to recognize patterns in the data. It uses a method called backpropagation to adjust its weights and biases based on prediction errors.

Testing the Model: Following training, the model is tested. The testing data is fed into the model for predictions, which are then compared with actual values to assess the model's performance.

Evaluating the Model: Model evaluation involves metrics like Mean Squared Error (MSE), Mean Absolute Error (MAE), or Root Mean Squared Error (RMSE). These metrics offer a numerical measure of the model's performance.

Tuning the Model: If the model's performance is unsatisfactory, it can be adjusted by changing parameters such as the learning rate, number of layers, and neurons per layer.

Making Predictions: Once the model has been trained, tested, and tuned, it can be used to predict future stock prices using the most recent data.

Regular Updates: Regularly retraining neural network models with the latest data maintains their accuracy. Ensure your model is updated periodically.

Avoid Overfitting: Techniques like regularization, early stopping, or dropout can be used to prevent overfitting, which is when the model becomes excessively familiar with the training data and performs poorly on new data.

Use of Indicators: Including other indicators such as moving averages, relative strength index (RSI), and trading volumes in the dataset can enhance prediction accuracy.

Ensemble Models: Prediction accuracy can be improved by combining different neural network models, an approach known as ensemble methods.

Use of Time Series Forecasting: Techniques like Autoregressive Integrated Moving Average (ARIMA) or Long Short-Term Memory (LSTM) can be used since stock prices are time series data.

Handling Market Volatility: Methods like volatility modeling or using models that can capture non-linear relationships in the data can ensure your model is robust enough to handle market volatility.

Handling Data Non-stationarity: Techniques like differencing or transformations can be used to make non-stationary stock data, whose statistical properties change over time, stationary.

Limitations: Despite their capabilities, neural network models are not infallible and can make incorrect predictions. Understanding these limitations and not relying solely on these models for trading decisions is critical.

Patience and Persistence: Lastly, remember that building an effective stock prediction model requires time and persistence. Don't lose heart if your initial models don't perform well. Continually iterate and refine your models.

Situation:

John, a financial analyst at a top-tier investment firm, works to devise innovative strategies to predict stock prices and gain a competitive advantage. Recently, his firm has chosen to utilize a neural network model for forecasting stock prices.

Implementation Plan:

Data Gathering: John begins by amassing historical stock price data from different financial sites and APIs. His data includes open, close, high, and low prices, as well as trade volumes.

Data Cleaning: He eliminates any errors in the data and normalizes the numerical variables to a common scale before dividing the dataset into training and testing subsets.

Neural Network Design: John designs his neural network model, customizing the number of layers, neurons per layer, and activation functions to suit the stock data.

Training: The training data is input to the model, which learns to identify patterns. Prediction errors are corrected using backpropagation to adjust weights and biases.

Testing: Post-training, the model is evaluated using the testing data. The accuracy of the model's predictions are compared to actual values.

Evaluation: John assesses the model using metrics such as MSE, MAE, and RMSE.

Optimization: If the model's performance doesn't meet standards, John tweaks parameters like learning rate, number of layers, and neurons per layer.

Predictions: Once the model's performance is deemed satisfactory, John employs it to predict future stock prices using the latest data.

Regular Updates: John ensures the model is regularly retrained with the most recent data to maintain its accuracy.

Avoiding Overfitting: Techniques such as early stopping and dropout are used by John to prevent overfitting.

Indicators: The dataset is enhanced with indicators like moving averages, RSI, and trade volumes to improve prediction accuracy.

Ensemble Models: John integrates various neural network models to boost prediction accuracy.

Time Series Forecasting: As stock prices are time series data, methods like ARIMA or LSTM are utilized by John.

Market Volatility: To make the model resilient against market volatility, John employs volatility modeling.

Data Non-stationarity: Differencing or transformations are used by John to handle non-stationary stock data.

John recognizes the limitations of neural network models and doesn't use them as the sole basis for trading decisions. He demonstrates patience and persistence, constantly tweaking and improving his models for superior performance.

This text describes the typical steps involved in utilizing a neural network model for predicting stock prices.

Data Collection: For instance, let's say John collects data on a particular company's stock prices over the past five years. This data includes daily opening and closing prices, the highest and lowest prices, and the volume of trades.

Data Preparation: John then standardizes these values on a scale from 0 to 1. For example, if the data ranges from $100 to $200, a price of $150 would be standardized to 0.5.

Neural Network Configuration: John then constructs a neural network with five input nodes (representing the five data features), two hidden layers each containing ten nodes, and one output node (representing the predicted price).

Training: The neural network is then trained using the historical data. If, for instance, the stock price was $150 when the standardized opening price was 0.6, closing price was 0.7, high was 0.8, low was 0.5, and volume was 0.75, the network will adjust its weights and biases to predict a value close to 0.5 (the standardized price of $150) when it encounters these inputs.

Testing: Following training, John evaluates the model using a separate testing dataset, comparing the model's predicted prices with the actual prices.

Evaluation: Suppose the model has a mean absolute error (MAE) of 0.02. This indicates that, on average, the model's predictions deviate from the actual price by 2% of the price scale.

If the model does not perform satisfactorily, John can modify the model's parameters or incorporate additional features (like moving averages, RSI, etc.) and repeat the process.

Once the model performs satisfactorily, John can employ it to forecast future prices. For example, if tomorrow's opening, closing, high, low prices, and volume are 0.65, 0.68, 0.7, 0.64, and 0.8, respectively, and the model predicts a price of 0.66, then the forecasted price would be $166, assuming the price scale remains between $100 and $200.

Let's imagine that John is attempting to forecast the closing price of Company XYZ's shares for the upcoming trading day. He gathers five years' worth of historical data, which includes daily opening and closing prices, highest and lowest prices, and trading volumes. The data varies between $100 and $200. After pre-processing this data, John develops a neural network with five input nodes corresponding to the five features, two hidden layers each with ten nodes, and a single output node for the predicted price.

Here's a case study of how John might utilize this model for a prediction:

Data Collection: Let's say the opening prices for Company XYZ's shares over the last five trading days were $150, $152, $155, $160, and $162. The closing prices were $152, $155, $160, $162, and $165. The peak prices were $155, $158, $162, $165, and $168, while the lowest prices were $148, $150, $153, $158, and $160. The trading volumes were 1 million, 1.2 million, 1.5 million, 1.8 million, and 2 million shares.

Data Preparation: John normalizes these figures to a scale from 0 to 1. For instance, an opening price of $150 would be standardized to 0.5 ((150-100)/(200-100)).

Neural Network Configuration: John introduces the standardized data into the neural network as inputs.

Training: The network modifies its weights and biases based on the discrepancy between its projected closing price and the actual closing price each day.

Testing: Following training, John tests the model with a separate testing dataset.

Evaluation: Let's say the model has a Mean Absolute Error (MAE) of 0.02. This suggests that the model's predictions, on average, differ from the actual price by 2% of the price scale.

Making Predictions: John now employs the model to anticipate the closing price for the next trading day. Let's say the opening price is $165, the highest price is $170, the lowest price is $163, and 2.2 million shares are being traded. After standardizing these figures, John inputs them into the model, which forecasts a standardized closing price of 0.68. John then reverts this back to the original price scale, resulting in a projected closing price of $168 ((0.68*(200-100))+100).

Regular Updates: John consistently inputs new data into the model and retrains it on a regular basis to ensure its precision.

It's important to remember that this example is quite simplified. In reality, neural network models can be much more intricate, and forecasting stock prices is a complicated task that entails a high level of uncertainty.

Decision Tree Models

Probabilistic models are crucial in financial markets, particularly for predicting stock prices. A commonly used probabilistic model is the Decision Tree Model. This model utilizes a tree-like graph or model to illustrate a sequence of decisions and their potential consequences, including the outcomes of chance events, resource expenses, and utility. It's a way to present an algorithm that only includes conditional control statements.

Decision Tree Models are incredibly useful when dealing with extensive data. They allow traders and investors to make informed decisions by giving a detailed analysis of different outcomes based on diverse choices. This model aids in understanding how various factors can impact a stock's price.

In a decision tree model, each node represents a decision, and the branches from each node signify the potential results of that decision. The terminal nodes or leaves denote the final outcomes based on the series of decisions made. The path from the root to a leaf provides a possible scenario or outcome.

One of the primary benefits of using a decision tree model is its simplicity. It's easy to comprehend and interpret, even for those without a solid statistical background. It enables financial analysts and traders to visualize potential outcomes and make decisions that align with their investment objectives.

A decision tree model takes into account various factors such as past performance, economic indicators, and market sentiment when predicting stock market trends. It systematically simplifies the larger problem of predicting stock prices into smaller, more manageable problems.

The model is also capable of incorporating different types of data, including numerical data like previous stock prices, and categorical data like industry type or company size. This flexibility makes it a valuable tool in predicting stock prices.

Another key feature of decision tree models is their ability to manage non-linear relationships between parameters. This is particularly relevant in stock market prediction as relationships between variables are often complex and non-linear.

Also, decision tree models are non-parametric, which means they don't make assumptions about the underlying data distribution. This is a crucial feature as stock market data often does not follow a normal distribution.

However, decision tree models are not without limitations. They can overfit or underfit data. Overfitting occurs when the model also captures the noise in the data along with the underlying pattern. Underfitting happens when the model doesn't capture the underlying pattern in the data.

To counter these problems, techniques like pruning, setting the minimum number of samples required at a leaf node, or setting the maximum depth of the tree are used to optimize the model and enhance its predictive power.

Unfortunately, decision tree models do not take into account the time-series nature of stock market data. This is a significant drawback as stock prices are heavily time-dependent. Techniques such as rolling window analysis and recursive partitioning can be used to address this issue.

Despite these limitations, decision tree models continue to be a widely used tool for predicting stock prices. Their simplicity, flexibility, and ability to manage complex non-linear relationships make them a valuable tool in the financial markets.

Decision tree models have become a popular tool in the financial industry, particularly for predicting stock market trends. These models harness past data to forecast future stock prices. This guide explains how to use this approach for predicting share prices in the stock market.

Firstly, it's important to understand what a decision tree model is: it's a visual depiction of all potential solutions or results that might arise from a sequence of decisions, consisting of nodes (which represent decisions or results) and branches (which represent the path between decisions).

To apply a decision tree model for share price prediction, you must first collect historical stock market data. This data is crucial as it underpins your predictions. You can source this data from financial platforms such as Yahoo Finance, Google Finance, or Bloomberg.

After obtaining the data, the next step is data preparation, which includes cleaning the data, handling missing values, and reformating the data into a format that the decision tree model can interpret. This step is vital as the quality of your data influences the accuracy of your predictions.

Next, you need to select the features or variables for your model. These might include past stock prices, trading volume, company earnings, or economic indicators. The selected features should significantly influence the stock price.

After selecting the features, split your data into a training set and a testing set. Use the training set to develop the model, and the testing set to assess the model's performance. It's common to allocate 70-80% of the data for training and the remaining 20-30% for testing.

You can now construct your decision tree model using the training data. Various algorithms, such as ID3, C4.5, and CART, are available for this purpose. These algorithms employ different methods to build the tree and segment the data.

Constructing the decision tree involves making decisions at each node based on the features, using criteria like information gain or gini index. The goal is to facilitate splits that result in the most homogeneous branches.

Once the decision tree is constructed, you can start making predictions. This process starts at the tree's root and involves making decisions based on the new data's features until you reach a leaf node, which represents the predicted stock price.

After making the predictions, assess the model's performance by comparing the predicted stock prices with the actual prices in the testing set. Evaluation metrics commonly used include mean squared error, root mean squared error, and R-squared.

If the model's performance doesn't meet your expectations, refine the model by adjusting its parameters. This can include the tree's maximum depth, the minimum number of samples required to split a node, and the number of features to consider when seeking the best split.

You might also consider trying different decision tree algorithms to enhance the model's performance. Each algorithm has its pros and cons, and the choice of algorithm depends on your data's specific traits.

You can also improve the model's performance by using ensemble methods like Random Forest or Gradient Boosting, which combine numerous decision trees to yield more accurate predictions.

Bear in mind that like any machine learning model, the decision tree model isn't flawless. Therefore, it should be used as a tool for making informed decisions rather than being the sole decision-maker.

It's crucial to remember that stock market predictions are inherently uncertain due to the numerous factors affecting stock prices. Therefore, understanding your model's limitations and considering other factors that might influence stock prices is crucial.

Finally, always keep your model current by training it with the latest data. This ensures that your model stays in tune with the latest trends and patterns in the stock market.

Scenario:

Imagine you're an investor aiming to forecast the future stock prices of a tech firm, "TechCo."

Strategy:

Data Collection: Begin by gathering historical share market records of TechCo from resources such as Yahoo Finance or Bloomberg. This may consist of past share prices, trading volume, company earnings, and other pertinent economic indicators.

Data Preparation: Cleanse and manage any incomplete data. Convert the data into a format that the decision tree model can read.

Feature Selection: Select the features or variables that significantly impact TechCo's share price. This may involve past share prices, trading volume, and company earnings.

Data Splitting: Partition the data into a training and a testing set. Allocate about 70-80% of the data for model training, and the remaining 20-30% for testing the model's effectiveness.

Model Construction: Create the decision tree model using the training data. You may employ algorithms like ID3, C4.5, or CART to construct the tree and segment the data.

Prediction: Once the decision tree is built, employ it to forecast TechCo's future share prices.

Model Evaluation: Compare the forecasted share prices with the actual prices in the testing set. Use evaluation metrics such as mean squared error, root mean squared error, and R-squared to measure the model's performance.

Model Refinement: If the model's performance is not up to par, enhance it by adjusting its parameters or experimenting with different decision tree algorithms.

Ensemble Methods: Think about using ensemble methods such as Random Forest or Gradient Boosting to boost the model's effectiveness. These methods merge multiple decision trees to provide more precise forecasts.

Continuous Training: Ensure that your model remains current by training it with the most recent data. This guarantees that your model remains aligned with the latest trends and patterns in the share market.

The strategy outlined above is essentially qualitative. However, using a straightforward probabilistic example, one can comprehend the procedure of forecasting stock prices. Suppose we use Earnings Per Share (EPS), a historically significant factor influencing stock prices, as the criteria for our decision tree.

Based on historical data, we know that:

When EPS was more than 5, the stock price rose 80% of the time. When EPS was 5 or less, the stock price fell 70% of the time. With this data, we can build a basic decision tree: If EPS > 5, we predict a rise in the stock price. If EPS <= 5, we predict a drop in the stock price. So, using this model, if we have a new EPS data point of 6, we would forecast an 80% probability of a stock price rise. Similarly, if the EPS is 4, we would forecast a 70% probability of a stock price drop.

This is a simplified example. Real-world situations would take into account numerous variables and utilize complex algorithms. For instance, a Random Forest algorithm would generate multiple decision trees, each taking into account different variables, and the final prediction would be based on the majority of votes from all decision trees.

It's important to remember that while decision trees are a good starting point, predicting stock prices is an extremely intricate process influenced by numerous unpredictable elements such as market sentiment, geopolitical events, and economic indicators. Hence, no model can guarantee absolute accuracy.

We'll use a basic example to demonstrate how a decision tree can help forecast stock prices. We'll continue our discussion using "TechCo" as our example company. Let's say we have five years' worth of data and want to forecast the stock price for the upcoming quarter.

The variables we'll take into account are:

Earnings Per Share (EPS)

The company's growth rate

The state of the economy (good, neutral, bad)

We'll begin by establishing decision nodes for each of these variables. The decision tree could look like this:

The first node is the EPS. If it's below 5, we forecast a decline in the stock price. If it's over 5, we move on to the second node. The second node considers the company's growth rate. If it's below 10%, we forecast a stock price decline. If it's over 10%, we move on to the third node.

The third node relates to the state of the economy. If it's bad, we predict a stock price drop. If it's neutral or good, we predict a stock price increase.

Let's say that currently, the EPS is 6, the company's growth rate is 12%, and the economy is doing well.

Based on our decision tree model, we forecast that the stock price will rise in the upcoming quarter.

But what's the likelihood of this happening?

To estimate this, we require historical data on the frequency of stock price increases when these conditions were met.

Let's assume that for the past five years:

The stock price rose 80% of the time when the EPS was over 5.

The stock price rose 70% of the time when the company's growth rate was over 10%.

The stock price rose 60% of the time when the economy was good.

Considering these probabilities, we calculate the combined likelihood as follows:

0.8 (likelihood of price increase given EPS > 5) x 0.7 (likelihood of price increase given growth rate > 10%) x 0.6 (likelihood of price increase given a good economy) = 0.336 or 33.6%

Thus, according to our decision tree model and historical data, there's a 33.6% likelihood that TechCo's stock price will increase in the next quarter.

Keep in mind, this is an oversimplification. In reality, you'd want to consider more variables and use more advanced algorithms for your prediction. You'd also want to use measures of uncertainty to express the range of potential outcomes.

Support Vector Machine Models

Predicting stock prices in the stock market heavily relies on probabilistic models, one of which is the Support Vector Machine (SVM) model. This model, a potent tool in machine learning, is often used for different financial applications due to its ability to process high dimensional data, making it ideal for stock predictions that take into account a multitude of factors.
The SVM model, a binary classification model, classifies data into two groups based on historical information. It uses this historical data of stock prices to predict potential future increases or decreases in stock prices. The SVM model is built on the principle of structural risk minimization, ensuring the model's broad applicability.
One of its key features is segregating data into different classes by locating the hyperplane that maximizes the margin between these classes. This hyperplane is defined by a small subset of the training data known as support vectors, which are the closest data points to the decision boundary.
An advantage of SVM models is their resistance to noise and a tendency to not overfit, a common issue in financial data analysis. This makes SVM models reliable and precise compared to other probabilistic models. The SVM model also includes a unique feature called the "kernel trick," which allows it to convert input data into a higher dimensional space. The model can then locate the optimal hyperplane in this new space, a task that might not be possible in the original space. This versatility enables SVM models to handle complex financial data.
However, the SVM model's performance relies heavily on selecting the appropriate parameters, such as the penalty parameter and the kernel function parameter. Correct parameter selection is vital for precise predictions, necessitating the use of methods like grid search or cross-validation for parameter optimization.
SVM models do have their limitations. They struggle with large datasets due to increased training time. Furthermore, they do not offer probability estimates for their predictions, which could be a disadvantage in some financial applications.
Despite these limitations, SVM models have been effectively used in various financial tasks, such as predicting bankruptcy, analyzing credit risk, forecasting exchange rates, and predicting stock market

trends. They have shown promising results in all these applications.

For stock price prediction, the SVM model uses historical data to identify patterns and trends in the stock market, aiding in the prediction of future stock prices. This is particularly useful for investors and traders who rely on accurate forecasts to make informed decisions.

The SVM model can be combined with other probabilistic models, such as random forest or neural networks, to improve prediction accuracy. These hybrid models utilize the strengths of multiple models for enhanced overall performance.

This guide will walk you through the steps of utilizing the SVM for this objective.

The first step is to accumulate historical stock price data, which can be sourced from financial websites or downloaded from financial analysis platforms such as Yahoo Finance or Google Finance. Make sure the data you compile is accurate and pertains to the stock you wish to forecast. Include aspects like opening price, closing price, highest price, lowest price, and volume of transactions.

Once you have gathered the data, you need to pre-process it. This includes cleaning the data, dealing with missing values, and converting the data into a format that the SVM model can accept. Additionally, normalizing the data is crucial as SVM is not scale-invariant.

Next, you should develop features to be used as inputs in your SVM model. These could be technical indicators such as Moving Averages, Relative Strength Index (RSI), and MACD among others, aiming to find patterns or trends in the stock prices.

The next step involves splitting the data into a training set and a testing set, with a common practice being to allocate 70-80% of data for training and the remainder for testing. However, for time series data like stock prices, a chronological split is often more effective.

After preparing and dividing the data, you can begin constructing your SVM model. Python libraries like scikit-learn can be used to implement the SVM. The SVR (Support Vector Regression) function from this library can be used to predict a continuous variable like stock prices.

When starting the SVM model, a kernel function must be selected, which can significantly impact your model's performance. Commonly used kernels in SVM include linear, polynomial, and Radial Basis Function (RBF).

The linear kernel is often the choice for text categorization and other large-scale tasks. However, for predicting stock prices, the data is unlikely to be linearly separable, so other kernels might be more effective.

The polynomial kernel permits more complex transformations and can capture more complex relationships but it's computationally costly and may lead to overfitting if the degree of the polynomial is high.

The RBF kernel is a popular choice for SVM as it can map the data into an infinite-dimensional space and only requires one parameter, which can be helpful in discerning complex patterns in stock prices.

After choosing the kernel, the parameters of your SVM model need to be adjusted, including the C parameter, controlling the balance between achieving a low error on the training data and minimizing the norm of the weights, and the gamma parameter, defining how far a single training example's influence extends.

Following training the model, its performance needs to be assessed using metrics like Mean Absolute Error (MAE), Mean Squared Error (MSE), or Root Mean Squared Error (RMSE). Ensure to evaluate your model on the testing data to confirm it can generalize well to unseen data.

Once you're happy with your model's performance, it can be used to predict future stock prices. Bear in mind, however, that stock prices are influenced by numerous factors, some of which cannot be captured by historical data or technical indicators.

Remember that like any other model, SVM is not guaranteed to always generate accurate predictions. It's recommended to use the predictions from the SVM model in combination with other models or financial indicators for informed decisions.

An example of utilizing SVM to forecast stock prices can be demonstrated as follows:

Suppose you are an investor with a keen interest in the technology sector, and you want to predict the future prices of Apple stocks.

Initially, you collect historical data about Apple's share prices from a trustworthy financial source like Yahoo Finance. The data you gather includes information such as the opening price, closing price, highest price, lowest price, and transaction volume.

Once the data is collected, you clean and preprocess it, handling any missing values and converting it to a suitable form for the

SVM model. The data is also normalized to ensure scale-invariance.

Subsequently, you generate features to be utilized as inputs in your SVM model. You might calculate moving averages, Relative Strength Index (RSI), and MACD amongst other things, searching for patterns or trends in Apple's stock prices.

The data is then divided chronologically, with the earliest 75% of data used for training and the remaining 25% for testing the model.

With your data ready, you begin building your SVM model using Python libraries such as scikit-learn. You choose the RBF kernel function as it is efficient in identifying complex patterns in stock prices.

You tweak the parameters of your SVM model, taking into consideration the balance between achieving a low error on the training data and minimizing the norm of the weights (C parameter), and determining how far the influence of a single training example extends (gamma parameter).

After training your model, you evaluate its performance using metrics like Mean Absolute Error (MAE), and Root Mean Squared Error (RMSE). You test your model on the testing data to verify its capability to generalize to unseen data.

If you're happy with the performance of your model, you use it to predict future prices of Apple's stocks. However, you understand that stock prices are greatly affected by various factors, some of which cannot be captured by historical data or technical indicators. As a result, you merge the predictions from your SVM model with other models or financial indicators to make wise investment decisions.

This is a useful method of employing SVM in real-time for forecasting stock market prices.

Consider this example, your historical data indicates that whenever Apple's stock price's 50-day moving average surpasses the 200-day moving average, there's a subsequent increase in the stock price over the following month. By training your SVM model with this historical data, it begins to recognize this pattern. Consequently, you can employ this model to forecast stock prices for the upcoming month. If the current 50-day moving average exceeds the 200-day moving average, the SVM model anticipates a price surge.

To work out the probability, let's assume that in the past 100 occurrences where the 50-day moving average was greater than the 200-day moving average, the stock price rose 70 times in the subsequent month. Therefore, the chance of the stock price rising, given that the 50-day moving average is above the 200-day moving average, is calculated as $70/100 = 0.7$ or 70%.

However, remember that this is a simplified scenario. In actuality, stock price prediction is a complicated process that necessitates analysis of multiple patterns and trends. Moreover, it's impossible to predict stock prices with absolute certainty due to the inherent unpredictability and volatility of the stock market.

To illustrate how Support Vector Machine (SVM) can be utilized in predicting stock prices with probabilistic measures, let's consider a hypothetical situation. Suppose you want to predict the stock prices of a tech company called XYZ Corp. You've gathered historical data from the past five years, including daily opening and closing prices, highest and lowest prices, and transaction volumes.

Once you've processed and cleaned the data, you calculate a few technical indicators, such as the 50-day moving average (50-MA) and 200-day moving average (200-MA). These moving averages are useful in identifying trends in stock prices.

Assume you've observed a pattern where the stock price tends to rise in the following month whenever the 50-MA exceeds the 200-MA. In the past five years, there have been 120 instances where the 50-MA was higher than the 200-MA, and in 84 of these instances, the stock price rose the next month.

Therefore, the likelihood of a price increase when the 50-MA is greater than the 200-MA can be calculated as follows:

P(Price increase | 50-MA > 200-MA) = Number of times price rose when 50-MA > 200-MA / Total instances when 50-MA > 200-MA = $84/120 = 0.7$ or 70%

Therefore, there's a 70% probability that XYZ Corp's stock price will rise over the next month when the 50-day moving average is greater than the 200-day moving average.

After training your SVM model with this historical data and choosing the right kernel function and parameters, you can use the model to predict if the stock price will rise in the next month, based on the current 50-MA and 200-MA values.

Keep in mind that this is a highly simplified example, and various other factors can affect stock prices. Nonetheless, this scenario provides an insight into how SVM can be paired with technical indicators to predict stock prices.

Reinforcement Learning Models

In the financial sector, probabilistic models, especially the Reinforcement Learning Model, are essential tools for predicting stock market trends. Reinforcement Learning (RL) is a method of machine learning that allows an algorithm to interact with an environment, generating actions and identifying errors or rewards. When utilized in the stock market, it can aid in predicting price trends and making trading decisions based on future rewards maximization.

RL models are particularly helpful in predicting stock prices due to their ability to make decisions based on long-term outcomes, a critical feature considering the dynamic and continuously evolving nature of stock markets. Traditional prediction models often fall short in this regard as they focus mainly on short-term predictions.

In the context of stock market prediction, the RL model learns to trade stocks based on historical price data, continuously evolving its trading strategy based on the rewards (profits) and penalties (losses) it receives. Its objective is to maximize cumulative rewards while minimizing penalties.

The RL model works on the concept of states, actions, and rewards. For example, in stock market prediction, a state could be the current stock price, the action could be buying, selling, or holding the stock, and the reward could be the profit or loss resulting from the action.

The model learns the optimal policy by exploring different actions in different states and observing the resulting rewards. Over time, it learns to link certain actions with higher rewards in certain states, thus enhancing its trading strategy.

One of the benefits of RL models is their capability to handle large state and action spaces, which is particularly helpful in stock market prediction where the number of possible states (combinations of stock prices) and actions (buy, sell, hold decisions) can be vast.

Furthermore, RL models can adapt to changes in the stock market, learning and adjusting their trading strategies based on new information, making them suitable for the unpredictable nature of the stock market.

However, RL models do come with their set of challenges. Their performance can be influenced by the quality and quantity of training data. Also, the reward function, which calculates the profit or loss from an action, can be challenging to define in a stock market scenario.

In the realm of stock market forecasting, the agent refers to a decision-making algorithm based on input data. The first step is understanding your environment, which in a stock market context, includes current and historical stock prices, volume, market indicators, etc. The detailed the data, the better the reinforcement learning algorithm can predict future prices.

Next, determine the state of your environment, which in reinforcement learning refers to the agent's current situation. For stock market forecasting, the state could include the current share price, its historical performance, or any other relevant data point. The third step is defining the actions your agent can take, such as buying, selling, or holding a stock, each with its own reward or punishment. The reward function is set for the agent, which could be a profitable trade or a loss-making one. The aim is to train the agent to maximize rewards over time, thus maximizing profits and minimizing losses in the stock market.

Choosing the right reinforcement learning model is important, with popular models including Q-Learning, Deep Q-Network (DQN), and Policy Gradients. Your choice depends on your specific needs and resources.

The training process involves letting the agent interact with the environment, make decisions and learn from the results. The agent uses these experiences to enhance its knowledge and decision-making abilities.

Ensure your model can cope with the stock market's unpredictable nature, influenced by various factors. Regularly evaluate your model by comparing its predictions with actual prices to ascertain accuracy. Backtesting is also essential before deploying your model, as is considering transaction costs and avoiding overfitting.

Using multi-agent reinforcement learning, which mimics the actual stock market where multiple traders interact simultaneously, can also be beneficial. Your model should be adaptable to the ever-changing stock market and new data. Reinforcement learning is not foolproof but can be a useful tool for predicting stock prices when used with other analysis techniques. Continuously refine your model as you gather more experience and data. Don't overlook risk management, stay updated with the latest developments in reinforcement learning, and be patient, as these models can take time to train.

Example Situation:

Imagine a fictitious company named "TechFirm". As an investor, your aim is to employ reinforcement learning to forecast the future stock prices of TechFirm.

Effective Approaches:

Data Accumulation: Collect extensive data pertaining to TechFirm. This can include their present and past stock prices, the quantity of shares traded, market indicators, earnings reports, news articles, and so forth.

Outline the Environment: The environment pertains to the stock market, incorporating all elements that impact the stock prices of TechFirm.

Establish the State: The state may be a mixture of the existing stock price, historical performance, the financial status of the company, or any other significant data points that may impact your decision.

Specify the Actions: The actions that your agent could perform are buying, selling, or holding TechFirm's stock.

Determine Rewards: Set a reward function for your agent. For instance, if the agent decides to purchase a stock and its price rises in the future, it receives a positive reward. Conversely, if the price decreases, it incurs a negative reward.

Select a Model: Based on your requirements and resources, select a reinforcement learning model. For example, the Deep Q-Network (DQN) is capable of managing high-dimensional inputs, making it suitable for complex stock market data.

Training: Train your agent by letting it interact with the environment, make decisions, and learn from its actions.

Evaluation and Backtesting: Frequently evaluate the performance of your model by comparing its predictions with the actual stock prices. Backtest your model using historical data to ensure its effectiveness before implementing it for real-time trading.

Multiple Agents: Consider the idea of having multiple agents as it replicates the actual stock market where numerous traders are buying and selling concurrently.

Continuous Improvement: Continually refine your model as you collect more data and gain more experience. The stock market is volatile and changes frequently, thus your model should be capable of adapting to these changes.

Risk Management: Do not neglect the risks associated with stock trading. Establish limits to manage potential losses.

Calculation of a Hypothetical Scenario:

Consider a basic situation where we employ a Deep Q-Network (DQN) to anticipate the future stock prices of TechFirm. We have three potential actions: purchasing, selling, or retaining the stock.

Presume the present situation is depicted by a vector which includes the current TechFirm stock price ($100), the average price from the last 10 days ($95), and a binary variable indicating whether a significant news article was published today (1 for yes, 0 for no). Today's news is positive (1).

The DQN forecasts the Q-values for the three actions based on the current state. Let's say the Q-values are 10 for buying, -5 for selling, and 0 for holding. Based on these predictions, the DQN recommends purchasing the stock as the best action.

You purchase the stock and the next day, the stock price increases to $110. This results in a reward of $10 (110-100). This positive reward will be used to refine the DQN and enhance its future predictions.

To mitigate risk, you could establish a cap on the maximum amount of money you're prepared to lose in a single trade. For instance, if the limit is $5, you would sell the stock if the price falls to $95 (100-5).

In a scenario with multiple agents, each agent could have different states and make different decisions. For example, another agent might have a state suggesting that the price has been falling over the past 10 days and decide to sell the stock instead.

These decisions and their results (rewards) would be used to consistently train and refine the agents, enabling them to adjust to new market conditions and hopefully provide more accurate predictions over time.

Let's examine a situation where the TechFirm stock price has varied over a span of 10 days at these rates: $90, $92, $95, $91, $93, $96, $94, $98, $96, and $100. We can choose from three actions: purchase, sell, or retain. We can identify the state as an array of the prices from the last 5 days. For instance, the state on day 6 would be [$90, $92, $95, $91, $93].

Assuming we have a trained DQN model capable of predicting the Q-values (or anticipated future benefits) for each action based on a state. On day 6, the DQN predicts Q-values as follows, given the state [$90, $92, $95, $91, $93]: 5 for purchasing, -3 for selling, and 0 for retaining. This suggests that purchasing will yield the highest future benefit, according to the DQN's prediction, so we opt to buy the stock at $96.

The following day, the stock price rises to $98. Since we bought the stock, our benefit (profit) is $2 ($98 - $96). This benefit is then used to update the DQN's predictions. The DQN should ideally become increasingly proficient at predicting which action will yield the highest benefit as it receives feedback from an increasing number of actions.

Let's now consider a strategy for managing risk. Let's say we're willing to risk a $3 loss on any single trade. We would sell the stock to limit our losses if the stock price fell to $93 the next day, resulting in a -$3 benefit.

In the case of multiple agents, each could have a different state and make a different decision. For example, another agent might have the state [$92, $95, $91, $93, $96] and predict the Q-values as -1 for purchasing, 2 for selling, and 0 for retaining. In this scenario, the second agent would choose to sell the stock.

As these agents interact with the market and receive feedback from their actions, they will continue to learn and hopefully refine their trading strategies.

Convolutional Neural Network Models

The use of probabilistic models for stock price prediction has been a common practice in the financial industry for a long time. However, the emergence of machine learning and artificial intelligence has elevated this practice. A notable model that's becoming increasingly popular is the Convolutional Neural Network (CNN) model. Initially intended for image and video processing, this model has been repurposed to accurately forecast stock market prices.

CNNs are a specific deep learning algorithm that processes an input image, assigns significance to different elements in the image, and distinguishes them. Compared to other classification algorithms, the pre-processing requirement in a CNN is considerably lower. While traditional methods require manually engineered filters, CNNs can learn these filters or characteristics with sufficient training.

In terms of stock market prediction, the "image" refers to historical stock market data. The CNN processes this data to detect patterns and trends that may be undetectable or unrecognizable to human analysts. These patterns are then used to anticipate future stock prices.

CNNs are especially suited for stock market prediction due to their capability to identify patterns in time-series data. Given that stock market data is a prime example of time-series data, CNNs can be trained to recognize specific trends, like rising or falling stocks, cyclical patterns, and more.

Additionally, the use of CNNs is not restricted to forecasting stock prices. They can also predict other financial indicators, such as trading volumes, market volatility, and many others. This range of applications makes them a valuable resource for financial analysts and traders.

The effectiveness of a CNN in predicting stock prices largely hinges on the quality and volume of the training data. The more data the model has, the better it can detect patterns and make predictions. Thus, it's imperative for financial institutions to have access to extensive, high-quality data sets.

A primary advantage of CNNs is their ability to process large amounts of data more quickly than human analysts. This enables real-time predictions, which are crucial in the fast-paced stock trading environment.

Furthermore, CNNs have the ability to learn and adapt over time. As they're exposed to more data, they continually refine their understanding of the market behavior, thereby improving their prediction accuracy.

However, it's crucial to remember that CNNs, like all probabilistic models, are not infallible. They can make incorrect predictions, particularly during periods of extreme market volatility or unforeseen events. Hence, they should be used as one of many tools in a trader's toolkit.

Also, while CNNs can detect patterns and trends in stock market data, they can't provide reasons for the existence of these patterns. Thus, they should be used alongside other tools and techniques that can offer this context.

Convolutional Neural Networks (CNNs), a type of Artificial Neural Networks, have demonstrated efficacy in fields like image recognition and classification. However, their applications extend beyond these areas, including predicting stock market prices—a challenging task due to high volatility and numerous influencing factors.

The first stage of using a CNN for this purpose involves gathering stock market data, potentially via APIs provided by most stock exchanges. This data should encompass daily opening, highest, lowest, and closing prices, as well as daily trading volumes.

Following data collection, preprocessing is required. This involves data cleaning, handling missing values, and data normalization. Normalization scales the data to a small specific range, typically from 0 to 1 or -1 to 1.

The subsequent stage involves dividing the data into training and testing datasets. Approximately 80% of the data is typically used for training and the remainder for testing.

Once divided, the data needs to be reshaped into a 3D array format, compatible with CNNs. This array comprises the number of records, time steps, and indicators.

Upon reshaping, you can begin constructing the CNN model. This model contains various layer types, beginning with a Convolutional Layer that applies a filter to the input data. This layer is followed by others, such as ReLU (Rectified Linear Units) for non-linearity, and Max Pooling Layer for downsampling.

The number and types of layers used depend on the specific problem. For stock price prediction, experimenting with various architectures may be necessary to find the most effective one.

After constructing the model, it must be compiled, requiring definition of the optimizer and loss function. The optimizer minimizes the loss function, with common choices including Adam, SGD, and RMSprop. The loss function measures prediction error, with Mean Squared Error (MSE) commonly used for regression problems like stock price prediction.

Following compilation, the model is trained with the training data. The model learns to predict stock prices by minimizing the loss function via the optimizer.

Post-training, the model's performance is evaluated using the testing data. This involves predicting the stock prices of the testing data with the model and comparing these predictions to real prices.

The model's predictive accuracy can be enhanced through tuning, which involves adjusting parameters such as learning rate, number of layers, and nodes per layer.

Finally, the trained model is used to predict future stock prices. This requires inputting the necessary data into the model and obtaining the predicted stock price.

For example, suppose an investment firm wants to predict Tesla, Inc's future stock prices using a CNN model. They would follow these practical steps:

Data Gathering: First, the firm would collect historical data on Tesla's stock prices, including opening, highest, lowest, and closing prices, as well as daily trading volumes. This data can be obtained from APIs provided by NASDAQ, where Tesla is listed.

Data Preprocessing: Next, the firm would preprocess this data, which includes cleaning it to eliminate any errors or inconsistencies, dealing with missing values, and normalizing it to a certain range.

Data Splitting: The firm would then divide the data into training and testing datasets, using approximately 80% of the data to train the CNN model and 20% to test it.

Data Reshaping: The data would be reshaped into a 3D array format compatible with CNNs. This array would include the number of records, time steps, and indicators.

Model Construction: The company would then start constructing the CNN model, which would consist of a Convolutional Layer, followed by layers such as ReLU and Max Pooling Layer.

Model Compilation: The model would then be compiled. The firm would need to specify the optimizer and the loss function.

The optimizer could be Adam, SGD, or RMSprop, while the loss function could be Mean Squared Error (MSE).

Model Training: The model would be trained with the training data, learning to predict Tesla's stock prices by minimizing the loss function through the optimizer.

Model Evaluation: The model's performance would be assessed using the testing data. The firm would use the model to predict the testing data's stock prices and compare these predictions to the actual prices.

Model Tuning: The firm would fine-tune the model to improve its predictive accuracy, adjusting parameters such as learning rate, number of layers, and nodes per layer.

Future Predictions: Finally, the trained model would be used to predict Tesla's future stock prices. The firm would input the necessary data into the model to obtain the predicted stock price.

In this scenario, a company is seeking to forecast the next day's stock price for Tesla. They've gathered 60 days' worth of data, including opening, high, low, and closing prices, as well as daily trading volumes. The company has already carried out data preprocessing, splitting, reshaping, and model building. They've trained the model on 80% of the data and are now prepared to make predictions.

For the sake of simplicity, we'll assume the company's Convolutional Neural Network (CNN) model consists of a single layer that predicts a binary outcome: the stock price will either rise (1) or fall (0).

The last 60 days of data are input into the model, which then forecasts a probability distribution for the following day's price: a 65% chance of increase (P(up) = 0.65) and a 35% chance of decrease (P(down) = 0.35).

The company decides to predict a price increase if P(up) is more than 0.5. As a result, the model predicts that the price will rise the next day.

The company verifies the actual price the following day. If the price increased, the prediction was accurate; if it decreased, the prediction was not.

The company repeats this process daily, continuously updating the model with the latest 60 days' worth of data. Over time, the model learns from its errors and tweaks its parameters to improve its predictive accuracy.

The company also keeps track of the model's performance and adjusts its hyperparameters, such as learning rate, layer count, and nodes per layer, to further enhance its predictions.

Let's use an imaginary situation to demonstrate how CNN models can be used to predict stock prices. We'll look at a made-up company, XYZ Corp, and pretend we've been tracking its stock price for the last 60 days. To keep things straightforward, we'll only focus on the closing prices.

Suppose the closing prices for the past 60 days were as follows (in USD):

Day 1: 100

Day 2: 105

Day 3: 103

Day 4: 108

Day 5: 110

...

Day 60: 200

We would then process and normalize this data to a 0-1 scale. In our case, let's say the normalized prices range from 0.1 to 1.

The next step is reshaping this data into a 3D array that can work with CNNs. This array would include the number of records (60), time steps (1), and indicators (1).

We would then use our CNN model, which has been trained on similar data, to predict the closing price for Day 61. For simplicity, we'll say our CNN model has a single Convolutional Layer.

Our model predicts a 70% likelihood that the price will go up (P(up) = 0.7) and a 30% chance it will go down (P(down) = 0.3). Based on this, we predict that XYZ Corp's stock price will rise on Day 61.

If the actual closing price on Day 61 ends up being 202 USD, it would confirm our prediction of a price increase. This would mean our model was accurate in this case.

However, it's crucial to remember that this is a highly simplified example. Real-world stock price prediction involves complex models with multiple layers and numerous influencing factors. Also, while our example indicates that the model's prediction was accurate, CNN models, like all predictive models, aren't always right and their predictions should be used alongside other analysis techniques.

Part: Instances of Successful Forecasts Using Probability-Based Models

Black-Scholes Model

The Black-Scholes model effectively forecasts stock prices due to its strong mathematical groundwork. It presumes markets to be efficient and that financial returns adhere to a normal distribution, a belief widely recognized in financial academia. The model takes into account the likelihood of various price fluctuations, incorporating elements like the current stock price, the option's strike price, time until expiry, stock volatility, and the risk-free interest rate. The Black-Scholes model requires investors to input these five parameters. The resulting figure, generally known as the Black-Scholes value, symbolizes the theoretical fair value of a financial derivative. If the market price differs from the Black-Scholes value, investors might exploit this disparity for profit.

Let's depict this with some instances:

Consider an investor contemplating a call option for a stock trading at $50. The option's strike price is $52, with an expiry in 6 months. Assuming a risk-free interest rate of 5% and stock volatility of 30%, the Black-Scholes model would approximate the option price at around $4.04. If it's trading for more, it could be deemed overpriced and vice versa. In the Black-Scholes equation, these values would be inserted as: $S = \$50$, $X = \$52$, $T = 0.5$, $r = 0.05$, and $\sigma = 0.3$, resulting in a call option price (C) of $4.04. Now, consider a put option for the same stock, with identical parameters. The Black-Scholes model would approximate this option price at around $2.92. If it's trading for more, it could be viewed as overpriced and vice versa. Here, the values in the Black-Scholes equation would be: $S = \$50$, $X = \$52$, $T = 0.5$, $r = 0.05$, and $\sigma = 0.3$, resulting in a put option price (P) of $2.92.

Bear in mind that like all models, the Black-Scholes model operates on assumptions and hence isn't flawless. It assumes a constant risk-free interest rate and volatility, which might not always align with reality. However, it serves as a useful tool aiding investors in making informed choices about options trading. These examples should provide a clear understanding of how the Black-Scholes model serves as a probabilistic tool to evaluate stock prices.

Monte Carlo Simulations

Monte Carlo simulations have proven to be effective in forecasting stock prices due to their capability to take into account a variety of factors and uncertainties that could influence a stock's price such as economic indicators, corporate performance, market trends, and geopolitical events. These simulations use randomness to provide solutions to problems that could be deterministic in nature, thereby offering a more accurate and thorough prediction of possible outcomes.

To utilize Monte Carlo simulations, an investor first needs to pinpoint the factors that could impact the result of their investment like interest rates, inflation rates, and corporate earnings. These factors are then assigned a probability distribution based on either historical data or expert opinion. The simulations are run multiple times, each time randomly selecting a value for each factor from its respective probability distribution. The end result is a range of potential outcomes, each having its own probability.

To better understand how Monte Carlo simulation can be applied to predict stock prices, let's take a hypothetical scenario. Assume that you're contemplating investing in a specific company, XYZ. XYZ's shares are currently priced at $100, but you think that there are several elements that could influence this price in the next year. These elements include changes in interest rates, variations in the company's earnings, and shifts in market sentiment.

You have gathered historical data on these factors and used this data to create probability distributions. For instance, you might have discovered that the yearly interest rate has ranged from 1% to 5% in the past ten years, with an average of 3%. Similarly, the company's earnings have ranged from $2 to $6 per share, with an average of $4. Finally, you have discovered that market sentiment, measured by the price to earnings (P/E) ratio, has ranged from 10 to 20, with an average of 15.

With these variables and their respective distributions identified, you can now run a Monte Carlo simulation. In each simulation run, a random value is selected for each variable from its assigned distribution. These selected values are then used to compute a possible future share price for XYZ. This process is repeated numerous times, producing a range of possible future share prices.

Suppose we run the simulation 1,000 times. In one run, the interest rate might be 2%, the earnings $5 per share, and the P/E ratio 12, which might result in a future share price of $110. In another run, the interest rate might be 4%, the earnings $3 per share, and the P/E ratio 18, resulting in a future share price of $95.

After running the simulation 1,000 times, we might discover that the share price ranges from $80 to $120, with an average of $100. This range signifies the uncertainty surrounding the future share price, with each individual price within this range having its own probability of occurrence.

The investor can utilize this information to evaluate the risk and potential return of investing in XYZ. For instance, if the investor wants a return of at least 10%, they can check how many of the simulations resulted in a share price above $110. If this number is high, say 70%, the investor might decide to invest in XYZ. If the number is low, say 30%, the investor might decide to look for other investment opportunities.

Brownian Motion Model

The Brownian Motion model is a cornerstone in finance, particularly in forecasting stock prices. The model's effectiveness rests on the premise that stock price movements are random, meaning a stock's future direction doesn't depend on its past performance. This principle is based on the natural phenomenon known as Brownian motion, where particles in a fluid move randomly due to collisions with other particles.

The model excels in forecasting stock prices primarily due to its ability to factor in randomness and volatility - two prevalent characteristics in financial markets. It considers both the random shifts and the systematic risk of a stock. The Brownian Motion model is incorporated in the Black-Scholes model, a renowned option pricing model, to ascertain the theoretical price of financial derivatives.

Application of the Brownian Motion model involves some mathematical calculations. The future price of a stock is determined by its current price, the anticipated return (drift), the volatility (diffusion), and a random variable. The drift represents the average rate of return of the stock, while the diffusion signifies the standard deviation of the stock's returns. The random variable introduces unpredictability into the model, reflecting the unpredictable nature of financial markets.

To illustrate this, let's consider an investor who owns shares in a company, XYZ Inc., currently priced at $100. The annual expected return (drift) for the stock is 5%, and the volatility (diffusion) is 20%. The investor wishes to predict the stock price after one year.

Using the geometric Brownian motion formula, where $S(t)$ is the stock price at time t, $S(0)$ is the initial stock price, μ is the expected return, σ is the standard deviation of returns (volatility), and $W(t)$ is a random variable following a standard normal distribution.

For simplicity, let's assume the random variable $W(t)$ is 0. The formula simplifies to $S(t) = S(0) \, e^{(\mu - 0.5\sigma^2)t}$. Substituting the given values, we get $S(1) = \$100 \, e^{((0.05 - 0.5(0.20)^2)*1)} = \$104.02$. Thus, the investor can expect the stock price to be approximately $104.02 after one year.

But this is a simplified scenario. In reality, the random variable $W(t)$ won't be zero and will introduce an element of randomness to the stock price.

While the calculations may seem intricate, many financial calculators and software can do the math for you. What's crucial for an investor is to comprehend the underlying principle: the stock price's future direction doesn't depend on its past, and it factors in both systematic risk and random fluctuations. Remember, while the Brownian Motion model can offer a probabilistic evaluation of stock prices, it's not infallible. The model presumes that the markets are efficient, and it doesn't consider factors like market psychology or a company's fundamental analysis.

Autoregressive Integrated Moving Average (ARIMA)

ARIMA models have proven effective in predicting stock prices as they encapsulate a variety of standard time-based structures in time series data. The three components of these models are autoregression (AR), differencing (I), and moving average (MA). Autoregression is a model utilizing the dependent relationship between an observation and several previous observations. Differencing is applied to make the time series stationary, while the moving average model depends on an observation and a residual error from a moving average model applied to previous observations.

Investors can employ ARIMA models to analyze and forecast time series data such as monthly airline passenger numbers, daily temperatures, and stock prices, among other things. Understanding a stock's past price behavior and its influencing factors allows investors to make informed predictions about future trends and invest accordingly.

To illustrate, consider a scenario where an investor wants to predict the future stock prices of a company, XYZ, for the next 5 days and has the past 60 days of the company's stock prices.

Step 1: The investor first tests the stationarity of the time series data using an Augmented Dickey-Fuller test. If the time series is not stationary, it must be made so, as ARIMA requires stationary data. This can be done by differencing the data, that is, subtracting the value of the previous day from the value of the current day.

Step 2: After making the data stationary, the investor identifies the AR and MA terms using the AutoCorrelation Function (ACF) and Partial AutoCorrelation Function (PACF) plots.

Step 3: The investor then constructs the ARIMA model with the identified parameters and fits the model using historical data.

Step 4: The model can be validated by checking the residuals, which should ideally follow a normal distribution and have a mean of zero.

Step 5: The investor can now predict future stock prices using the model and also determine the confidence interval for these forecasts.

With the forecasted values and confidence intervals, the investor can decide whether to buy, sell, or hold the XYZ company shares.

However, it's crucial to remember that while ARIMA models can provide a probabilistic measure for assessing stock prices, they are not infallible. They assume that the future will mimic the past, which may not always be the case. Therefore, it's important to consider other fundamental and technical analyses along with this model. As always, remember that past performance does not guarantee future results.

GARCH Model

The GARCH model's success in predicting share prices comes from its ability to manage the inherent volatility of financial markets. This volatility often appears in clusters of high and low periods, something which conventional models find hard to encapsulate. This is where the GARCH model comes in, taking into account changing variances over time to better predict future price changes, using past volatility and errors.

This model is highly useful in financial markets where volatility plays a key role in decision making. It allows investors to gauge the risk of a potential investment. If an investment is highly volatile it's deemed risky, and this information allows investors to tailor their strategies based on the estimated volatility.

For a more detailed example, let's assume an investor is looking at investing in company XYZ, with access to the past 100 days of closing prices. They want to estimate the next trading day's volatility using the GARCH(1,1) model.

The first step would be to calculate the return series from the closing prices, the day-to-day percentage change in prices. The investor would then estimate the GARCH model parameters using this return series. The GARCH(1,1) model can be written as: $\sigma^2(t) = \alpha0 + \alpha1*\varepsilon^2(t-1) + \beta1*\sigma^2(t-1)$, where $\sigma^2(t)$ is the variance at time t, $\varepsilon^2(t-1)$ is the squared error from the mean at time t-1, $\sigma^2(t-1)$ is the variance at time t-1, and $\alpha0$, $\alpha1$, and $\beta1$ are parameters to be estimated.

Using statistical software, these parameters can be estimated. Let's say the estimated parameters are $\alpha0 = 0.0001$, $\alpha1 = 0.1$, and $\beta1 = 0.85$.

The investor can then use these parameters to estimate the next trading day's volatility. If, for example, the squared error from the mean on the last trading day was 0.002 and the variance was 0.01, the estimated variance for the next trading day would be: $\sigma^2(t) = 0.0001 + 0.1\times0.002 + 0.85\times0.01 = 0.009$. The volatility is then the square root of the variance, in this case approximately 0.095, indicating an estimated volatility for the next trading day of 9.5%.

This estimated volatility can be used to measure the risk of investing in company XYZ. A risk-averse investor might choose to avoid or lessen their investment in the company, while a risk-tolerant investor might choose to increase their investment.

LSTM (Long Short Term Memory) Models

LSTM (Long Short Term Memory) models have proven to be highly effective in forecasting stock prices due to their distinctive structure that enables them to 'remember' long-lasting trends and associations within data. This is particularly vital in stock price prediction, as prices are often impacted by a sequence of previous events and tendencies. Traditional stock price prediction methods, such as time series analysis, may overlook these long-term associations, leading to less precise forecasts.

LSTM models are specifically designed to tackle the long-term dependency issue by incorporating a type of memory. They possess a 'cell state', which acts like a conveyor belt, permitting information to flow through it with minimal alterations. It also includes 'gates' that manage the flow of information into and out of the cell state, ensuring that only pertinent information is preserved.

To employ LSTM models for predicting stock prices, an investor must first collect historical stock price data. This data is then split into training and testing datasets. The training data is used to educate the model, enabling it to comprehend the underlying patterns and dependencies. The testing data is used to assess the model's prediction performance.

After the data has been organized, the LSTM model can be assembled. This includes defining the network's architecture, such as the number of layers and units in each layer. The model is then educated using the training data, and its performance is assessed using the testing data.

Let's look at a detailed, computational scenario to better understand how LSTM models can be utilized for stock price prediction. For instance, an investor wants to predict the future price of a specific stock, like Apple Inc.

Initially, the investor gathers historical data of Apple's stock prices for the previous five years and separates this data into training and testing datasets. The first four years of data are used to train the model, and the final year is used for testing.

The investor then builds an LSTM model with two layers and 50 units in each layer. The model is trained on the training data using an appropriate optimization algorithm, such as stochastic gradient descent. This procedure involves repeatedly adjusting the network's weights to minimize the variance between the model's forecasts and the actual prices.

Once the model is trained, it is tested on the testing data. The model's predictions are compared to the actual prices to assess its prediction performance. If the model's predictions closely match the actual prices, this suggests that the model has grasped the underlying patterns in the data and can be used for future predictions.

The investor can then use the trained LSTM model to predict future prices of Apple's stock. These predictions can act as a probabilistic measure to evaluate the potential future performance of the stock. However, it should be noted that these predictions should not be the only basis for investment decisions. Other factors such as company fundamentals, market conditions, and economic indicators should also be taken into account.

Facebook's Prophet

The Prophet tool from Facebook has become popular in the financial sector, particularly in the stock market, due to its impressive capacity to forecast share prices. This is largely due to its effectiveness in managing time series data, which typically has a non-linear nature and a strong seasonal influence. Furthermore, the Prophet model takes into account the effects of holidays, which can greatly impact share prices.

The success of Prophet in predicting share prices is largely attributed to its additive model framework. This model breaks down a time series into three central components: trend, seasonality, and holiday effects. By separating these elements, the model can precisely capture any anomalies or changes in the data, thus enhancing its forecasting accuracy.

Using the Prophet model involves several steps for an investor. First, the investor must collect historical share price data, which the Prophet model will use for training. It should be noted that the model performs best with several seasons of data, so the more data provided, the better.

Then, the investor needs to implement the Prophet model in a Python or R environment. Once the model is in place, the historical data is input and the model is trained. After the training is complete, the investor can forecast future share prices.

For instance, if an investor has three years of daily stock prices for Company X and wants to predict the stock prices for the upcoming six months, they would begin by importing the necessary libraries in Python and loading the historical data. The data is then prepared by ensuring it is in the required format, a DataFrame with two columns: 'ds' for date and 'y' for stock prices.

The investor then creates an instance of the Prophet class and applies the historical data using the 'fit' method. The model learns the underlying patterns in the data.

In the next step, future predictions are made. The investor uses the 'make_future_dataframe' method to create a DataFrame for future predictions, setting the period to 180 days to forecast the next six months.

Once the future DataFrame is created, the investor uses the 'predict' method to make the predictions, which are usually in the form of a DataFrame with columns for the predicted values ('yhat'), as well as the lower ('yhat_lower') and upper ('yhat_upper') confidence intervals.

The investor can then display the predicted values using the 'plot' method, which provides a visual representation of the past and predicted stock prices. The actual prices are represented by black dots, the predicted values by a blue line, and the confidence intervals by a light blue shaded area.

The investor can also plot the forecast components using the 'plot_components' method, which provides insights into the data's trends and seasonalities.

Finally, the investor can use the predicted values and confidence intervals to make informed investment decisions. For example, if the lower confidence interval of the predicted stock price is higher than the current price, the investor might consider buying the stock.

However, it's important to remember that the Prophet model, like any forecasting model, isn't 100% accurate. It should be used alongside other investment tools and knowledge. Also, investors should always consider the inherent risks of the stock market.

About the Author

I am a professional research analyst and investor, holding an MBA in Finance and ACCA at the knowledge level. I have specialized in Google Digital Marketing & E-commerce, as well as Google Project Management. In addition to this, I have attended a day course on Social Sciences at the University of Oxford and a part-time course for three months on the same subject at the University of Cambridge. Furthermore, I have authored several books across various disciplines.

Azhar.sario@hotmail.co.uk

About the Publisher

I am a professional research analyst and investor, holding an MBA in Finance and ACCA at the knowledge level. I have specialized in Google Digital Marketing & E-commerce, as well as Google Project Management. In addition to this, I have attended a day course on Social Sciences at the University of Oxford and a part-time course for three months on the same subject at the University of Cambridge. Furthermore, I have authored & published several books across various disciplines.

azhar.sario@hotmail.co.uk